New CLAIT

Unit 5

Databases

The Course Book

CGP's Course Books offer a step-by-step approach to help you really get to grips with New CLAIT.

Each topic is explained using everyday language, with plenty of worked examples, handy hints and practical tasks.

Exactly what you need — perfect for even the most 'computer-phobic' learners.

Contents

Section One — Introduction

Section Two — Database Basics

Section Three — Entering and Amending Data

Section Four — Database Queries

Section Five — Managing Databases

Section Six — The Assessment

Published by Coordination Group Publications Ltd.

Contributors:
Jo Anson
Charley Darbishire
Dominic Hall
Simon Little
Rachel Selway
Jennifer Underwood

Endorsed by OCR for use with OCR Level 1 Certificate for IT users - New CLAIT specification

With thanks to Ray Davies and Kate Redmond for the proofreading.

ISBN 1 84146 327 2

Groovy website: www.cgpbooks.co.uk
Jolly bits of clipart from CorelDRAW
Printed by Elanders Hindson, Newcastle upon Tyne.

With thanks to Microsoft for permission to use screenshots from
MS Access XP and MS Windows XP.

What is New CLAIT?

Here's a page to let you know what this book is all about.

New CLAIT is a Computer Course for Beginners

In New CLAIT, you'll learn how to make computers work for you, so you can use things like:

- word processors — to write letters
- spreadsheets — to do your household accounts
- databases — to organise information
- e-mail — to keep in touch with people all over the world

Just Have a Go, You Won't Break it

The key to learning about computers is to try things.
Don't be afraid of it — you won't break the computer with a mouse and keyboard.
You'd need to open it up and pour a cup of tea inside to break it.

This book will take you through everything step-by-step. You'll be doing things all the time.

When you've got to do things, you'll find numbered shapes like this.

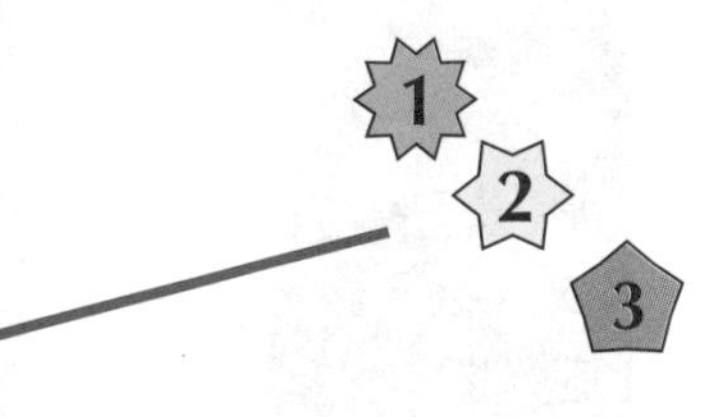

There are also practice exercises at the end of each section, so you can see how you'd do in a real New CLAIT test.

Read this bit if you are a Tutor

1) We've used Office XP and Windows XP Professional. This comes with Access 2002 which does look quite different to earlier versions but most things work in much the same way.
2) To keep things simple we've concentrated on one way of doing things instead of confusing people with five different ways to do the same thing.
3) There is a CD which accompanies this series of books. It contains all the files the student will need for the worked examples, practice exercises and exams. It also contains sample answer files for most of the exercises. The files have been saved in both .csv and .xls formats. They have also been saved in Microsoft Access in both 97 and 2000 formats.

Relax — computers are friendly...

This book tells you everything you need to pass New CLAIT Unit 5.
So just relax, have a go and enjoy it — you won't break your computer by just giving it a try.

The Bits of a Computer

This is a really straightforward page to remind you of all the different bits of a computer and what they do. A second or two's glance should do the job.

The Parts of a Computer Do Different Jobs

Here's a computer — and all the bits are labelled.

System box — the 'brain' of the computer, where all the bits and pieces that make it work can be found. You put CDs and disks in here, and plug all the other computer parts into the back.

Monitor — looks like a TV screen. What you're working on is displayed on it.

Printer — used to make a paper copy of what's on your screen.

CDs and floppy disks — can be used to store your work. You can put them into a different computer and your work will appear.

Mouse — when you move this over your desk, a little arrow on the screen will move too. You can use it to select and change different things on the screen.

Keyboard — has keys with letters and numbers on that you press to enter information, e.g. to write a letter.

I'm guessing you've seen this before...

I reckon it's unlikely that you are learning databases but don't know what the different parts of a computer are — so feel free to skim through, but there's never any harm in a quick reminder.

The Bits of a Computer

You know what the different bits of a computer are called, but there's a bit more to learn yet...

Computers come in Different Shapes

Laptops are handy little computers that you can fold up, carry about in a bag and use on the train, should you fancy. They're as good as normal computers, just smaller.

Notebooks are like laptops, but smaller and a bit less powerful. (Still plenty good enough for us normal folks though.)

Computers are made of Hardware and Software

HARDWARE is all the physical bits of a computer — not just the obvious bits like the monitor, keyboard and printer, but also the gubbins inside that make it work.

SOFTWARE is all the programs in a computer that make it do different things — i.e. the instructions that tell the computer what to do. You can buy new software on CDs.

For example, Microsoft Word is a program which lets you write letters and things. A computer game is another program, where the keys you press might guide a character round a special world. Nice.

Here are Some Terms You'll Need to Know

1) Programs, like Word or Excel, are called applications.
2) Files are made with applications. They contain the things you make — a file from a word processor, like Word, will be lots of text, and a file from a drawing program will be a picture.
3) A folder is a place where you can store files or applications. They're really useful for organising your computer.

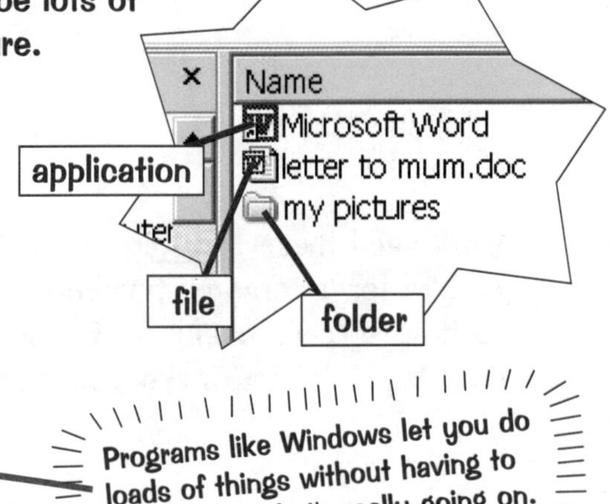

Windows is a special program called an 'operating system' — it lets you interact with the computer, open and close other programs, and generally control what's going on — useful.

Programs like Windows let you do loads of things without having to understand what's really going on.

This is all just a bit of useful background...

The different types and parts of a computer are useful background information.
If you get it straight in your head it'll make the whole business of databases a lot easier.

Using the Keyboard

I'm guessing you probably know the keyboard like the back of your hand — but just in case here's a quick whizz through the main bits...

All Keyboards Look the Same (More or Less)

The big bit with the letters on is always the same — it's the same arrangement as on a typewriter. So if you've used a typewriter before, you should pick it up really easily.

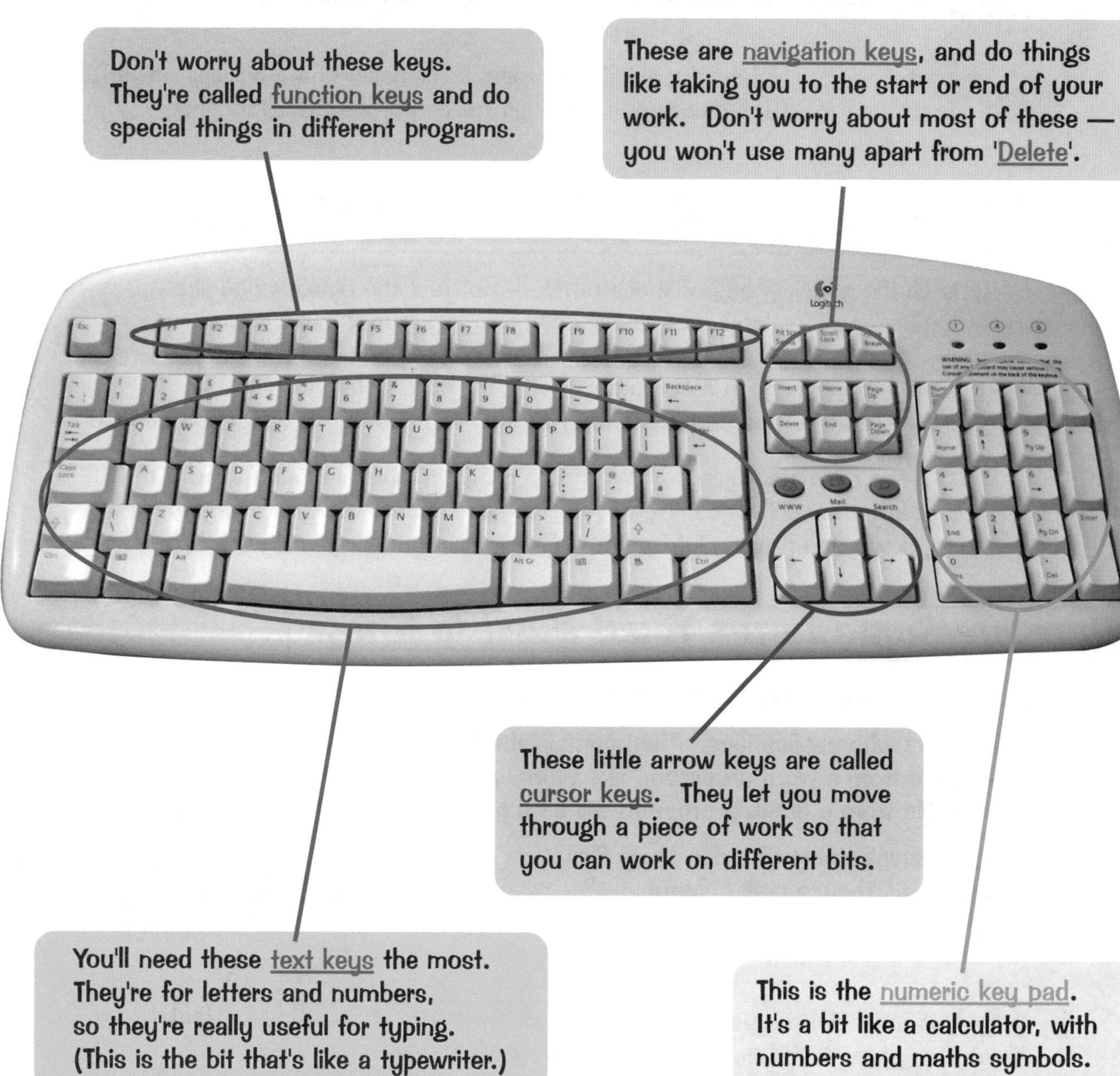

Don't worry about these keys. They're called function keys and do special things in different programs.
These are navigation keys, and do things like taking you to the start or end of your work. Don't worry about most of these — you won't use many apart from 'Delete'.
These little arrow keys are called cursor keys. They let you move through a piece of work so that you can work on different bits.
You'll need these text keys the most. They're for letters and numbers, so they're really useful for typing. (This is the bit that's like a typewriter.)
This is the numeric key pad. It's a bit like a calculator, with numbers and maths symbols.

The key to success — learn your keys...

Learning how to use a keyboard isn't hard. It's all those extra keys you don't need that make it look scary. But you're probably well past being fazed by that — so read on...

Using the Keyboard

Just in case you've forgotten what any of the keys do, here's a quick reminder.

Some Keys are Really Special

Here's some of the keys you'll find really useful when you're typing:

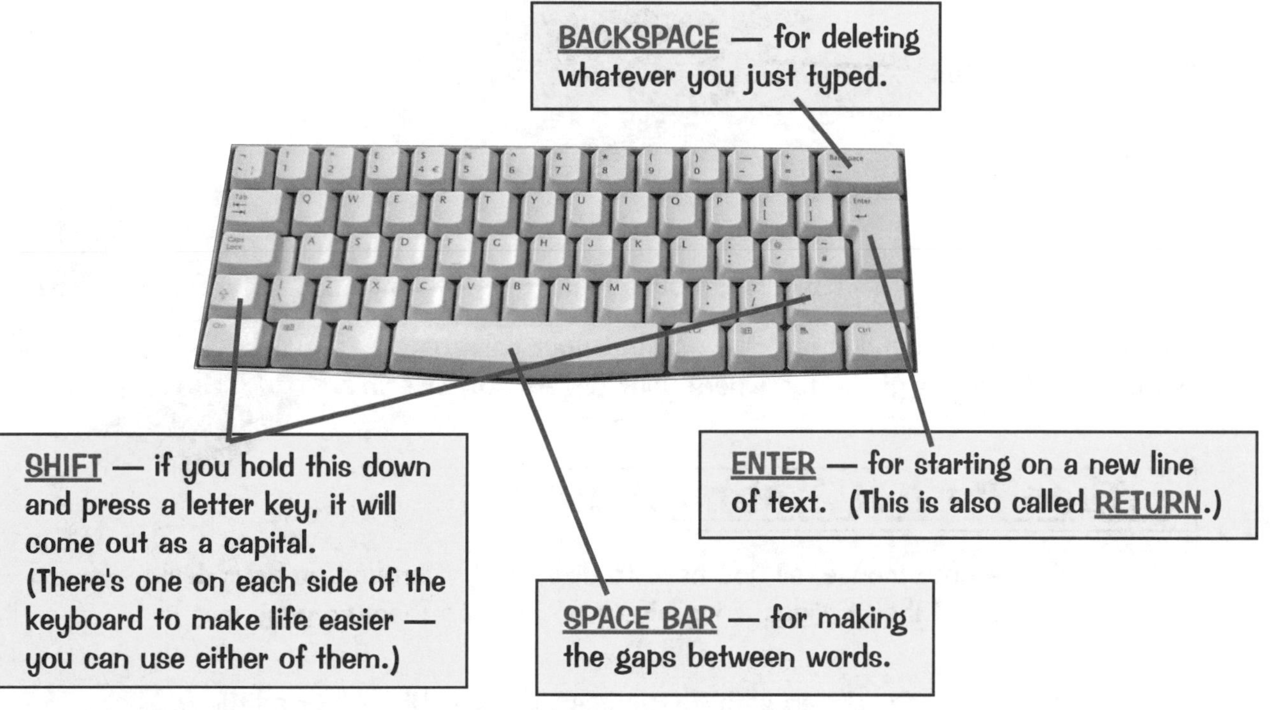

BACKSPACE — for deleting whatever you just typed.
SHIFT — if you hold this down and press a letter key, it will come out as a capital. (There's one on each side of the keyboard to make life easier — you can use either of them.)
ENTER — for starting on a new line of text. (This is also called RETURN.)
SPACE BAR — for making the gaps between words.

Have a Go at Using the Keyboard

Learning to type is really slow to begin with, but you'll soon get better with practice.
If you need a bit more practice, have a look at New CLAIT Unit 1 — Using a Computer.

Open a word-processing application and have a go at typing:

- Make sure you're typing accurately. It doesn't matter if you're slow.
- You don't have to whack the keys — find out how lightly you can press a key and still make it work.
- Make sure you know how to use the four special keys above.

After this I can teach you to suck some eggs...

OK, OK — you know all this already, so race on to Section Two — but if you realise that you have forgotten any of these little basics, you know where to look.

Get Used to the Mouse

You've probably got the mouse sussed by now — but it's so important it's worth a quick reminder...

First, Catch Your Mouse...

This is a mouse.

This is its right button (which you won't need for now).

This is its left button.

This is a mouse mat.

The mouse has a nice rounded top that you put your palm on, and a couple of buttons at the top where your fingers go. Like this:

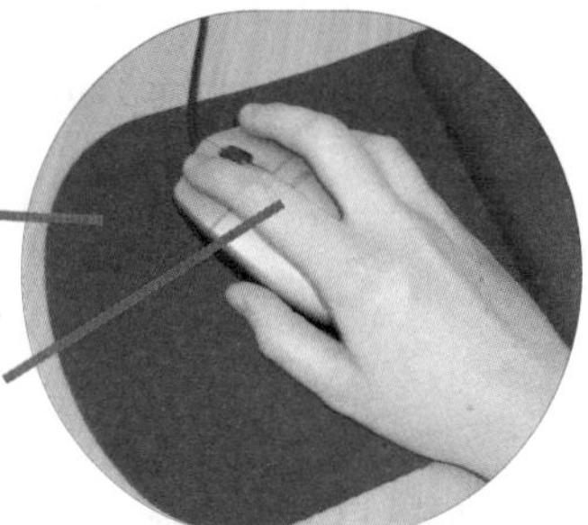

...Then Push it Around a bit

1) To use your mouse, all you have to do is push it around on your desk. (You'll find that it glides along nicely on top of a foamy mouse mat.)

2) Underneath the mouse will be a little ball or a little red light. This bit tells the computer how you are moving the mouse.

3) As you move the mouse, a little arrow on your screen moves about. This arrow is called a pointer.

Pointers look a bit like this. (But they're about ten times tinier.)

When you're using writing software, like Word, your pointer will look like this, but a lot smaller.

Don't worry if your pointer looks different to the ones above. It'll be really obvious — the pointer is the thing that moves about on your screen when you move the mouse.

Still trying to feed it cheese...

If you've been feeding your mouse cheese since you started CLAIT you've probably figured out it ain't hungry. The really astute may have noticed it has no mouth — some may have actually worked out how the mouse works. But all of you are sure to be bored of these gags by now.

Get Used to the Mouse

And now, following on from how to spot a mouse, how to use it properly.

You'll need to use the Left Mouse Button all the time

You normally just 'click' the mouse button — give it a quick press and then take your finger off again — you'll hear a little clicking noise.

- The left mouse button can 'select' things. This means that when you move the pointer over something and click your left mouse button, you'll make it 'alive' and useable.
- If you 'double-click' the left mouse button — quickly click on something twice — you'll be able to open programs and make things work.

Try this Quick Activity for Learning Mouse Control

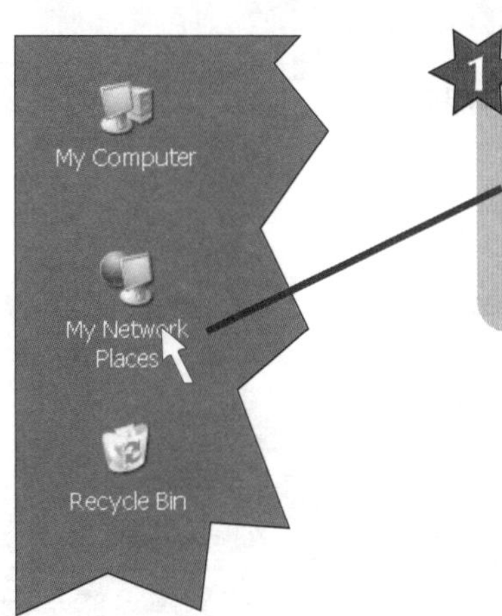

1

Move the mouse around until the pointer on the screen is on top of an icon. (An icon is a little picture, representing a file or application.)

2

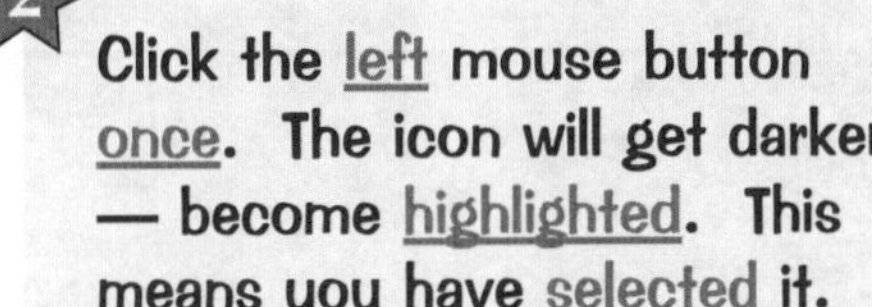

Click the left mouse button once. The icon will get darker — become highlighted. This means you have selected it.

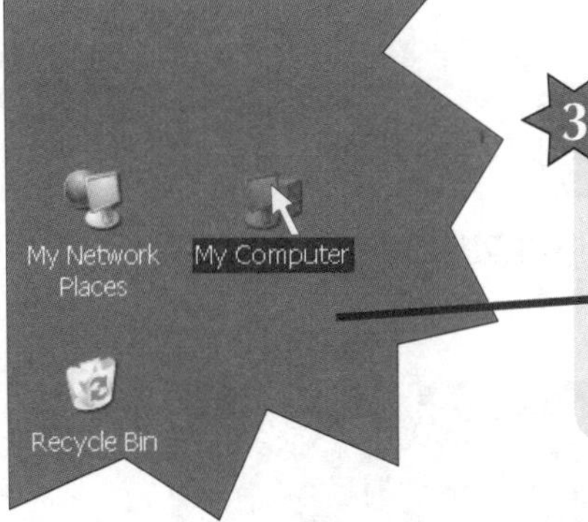

3

Move the pointer over a different icon. Press the left mouse button down and keep it held down. Then move your mouse and you'll find you can drag the icon about. Useful.

If you 'double-click' on an icon (move your pointer to it and do a quick 'click click'), you'll make it open.

That should have refreshed a few memories...

This little recap of computer basics should stand you in good stead. Refreshed with those vital basics it's time to get down to business, the business of databases. Hold on tight...

Databases

You're doing a module on databases, but do you really know what they are...

A Database is a Store of Data

1) A database is just an organised collection of data, like a set of record cards in a doctors' surgery. Each card contains information like name, address, phone number...

2) You can use a database to find out information about things, like the phone number of one of the patients at the surgery.

A Database is more Powerful than a Spreadsheet

You can use a spreadsheet like 'Microsoft Excel' as a database.

But if you're serious about organising your data, you'll probably need a database like 'Microsoft Access', or one of the other ones that are available.

There are some Obvious Differences

These are the main differences between a spreadsheet and a database:

SPREADSHEET

e.g. 'Microsoft Excel'

1) Doesn't save automatically, so data could be lost.
2) Easier to use than databases for fairly simple things.
3) Not easy to do more complicated things with the data.

DATABASE

e.g. 'Microsoft Access'

1) Saves automatically.
2) Can deal with lots of data.
3) Lots of tools for better inputting, editing, sorting and presenting of data.
4) Takes more time to set up.

Databases can do lots of Fancy Things

The benefits of a database are that you can search it quickly to find specific data, or use it to generate reports — e.g. which item in a shop has sold the most.

Some uses of databases

- Club or society membership records
- Employee records
- Sales and stock records in businesses

The database showed record sales figures for Balloons 'R' Us.

Databases are just amazing... honest...

You'll be amazed what you can do with a database. But for New CLAIT, you just need the basics — you don't even need to know how to create a new database, just how to use one.

Databases

'Microsoft Access' has lots of different ways for you to enter, process and present data, but don't be fazed — you just need to learn the basics for the assessment.

'Microsoft Access' looks like this:

Databases store basic data in tables. You'll learn more about them later in this section.

This database only has one table, called Table 1.

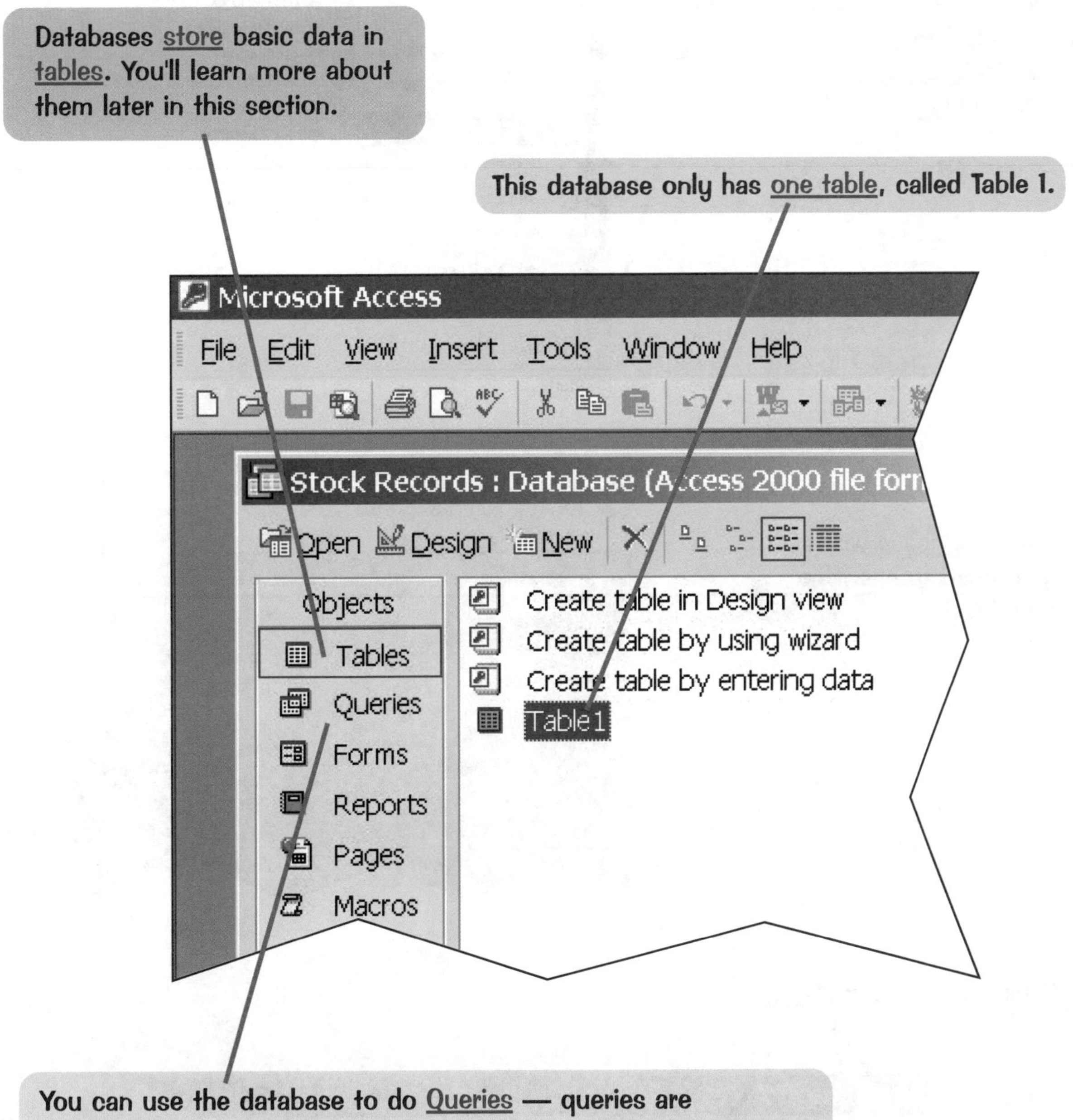

You can use the database to do Queries — queries are searches of the data. You'll learn more about them in section 4.

Don't worry, you'll learn how to open it in a minute...

Don't get too impatient — at least now you'll know what to expect when you turn over the page and get to open a database... if the excitement doesn't kill you first...

Opening Databases

The best way to learn about databases is to open one and have a look at it.

Opening 'Microsoft Access' is Easy

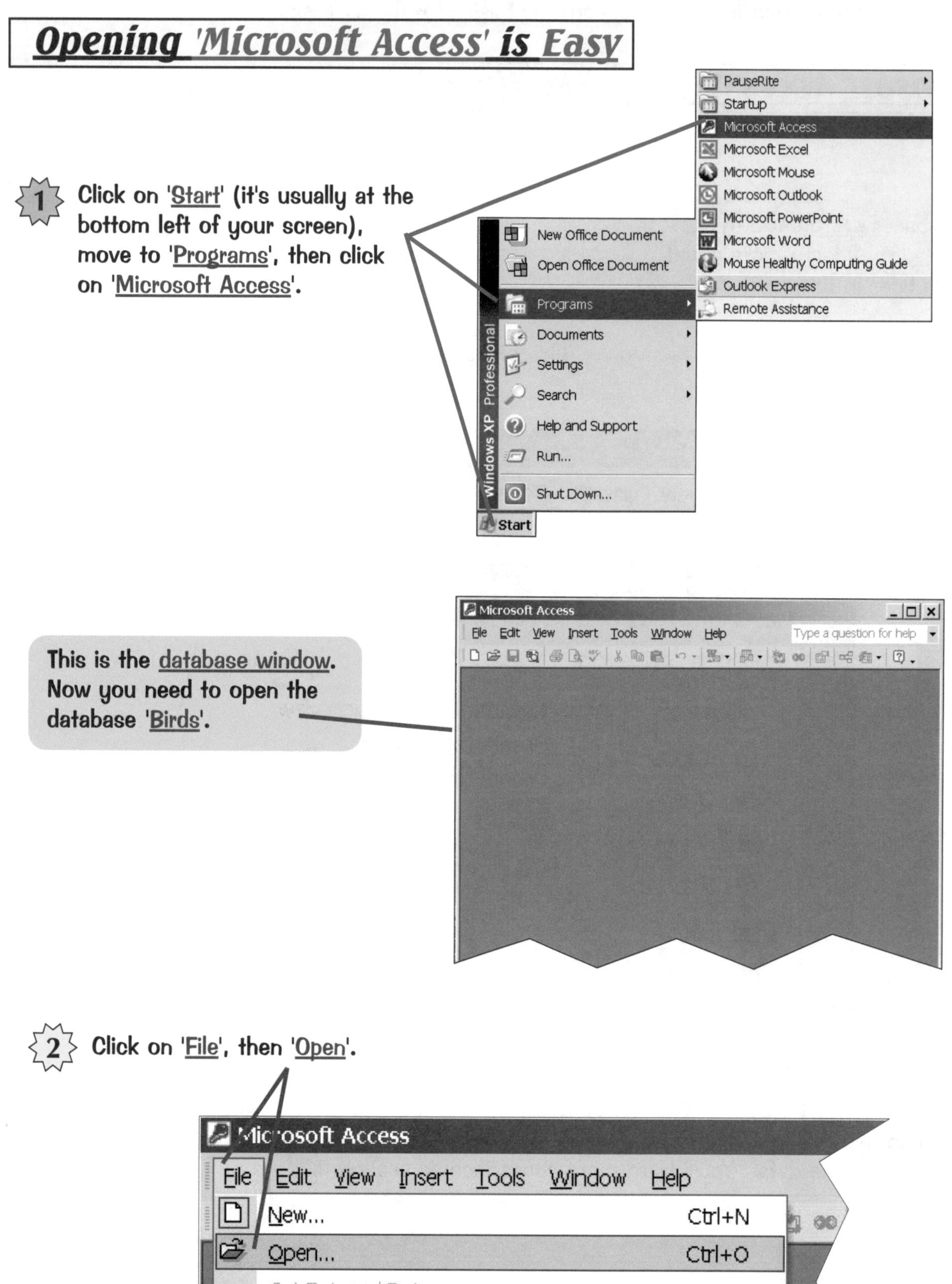

1. Click on 'Start' (it's usually at the bottom left of your screen), move to 'Programs', then click on 'Microsoft Access'.

This is the database window. Now you need to open the database 'Birds'.

2. Click on 'File', then 'Open'.

Opening Databases

Click on this arrow to look in other parts of your computer if you need to.

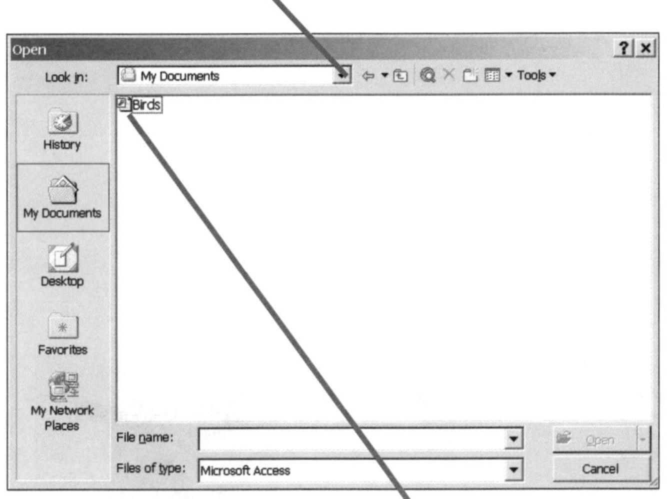

Move through the folders, double-clicking to open them.

The database 'Birds' is on the CD, so ask your tutor where to find it.

When you find the file 'Birds', double-click to open it. Hey presto — you've opened the database 'Birds'.

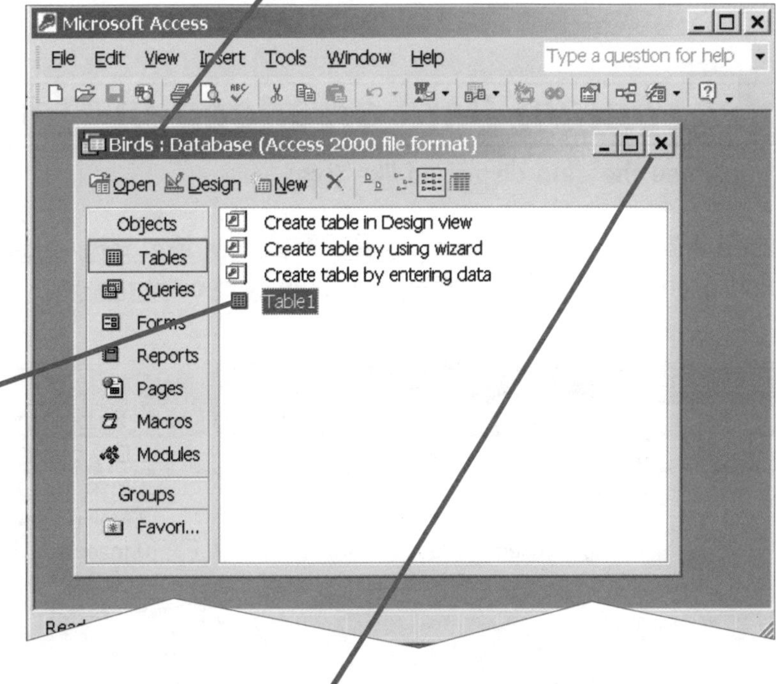

The actual information that a database contains is stored in separate tables like this (see the next page).

The databases in this unit are all nice and simple with only one table in them.

Click here to close the database 'Birds', but leave 'Microsoft Access' open.

Data, data everywhere...

Don't panic just because you think databases are complicated. You don't have to do anything very difficult to pass the assessment, so keep going and you'll soon be comfortable with them.

Database Basics

OK so you've opened a database, but where is all that data hiding?

The Data is Stored in Tables

To look at all the data, you need to open a table:

Open the database 'Birds' (see pages 10-11 for help).

Double-click to open Table 1.

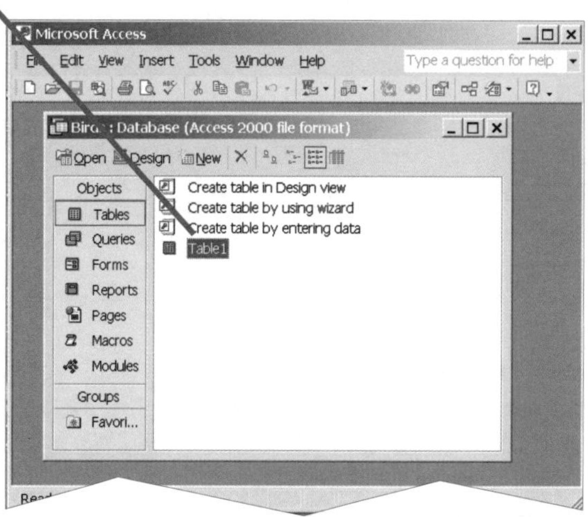

Not as good for storing data.

Tables contain Data arranged in Fields and Records

Now you'll see the data displayed like this:

Each column is called a field. These fields are like categories which divide up the data. They can hold text or numbers.

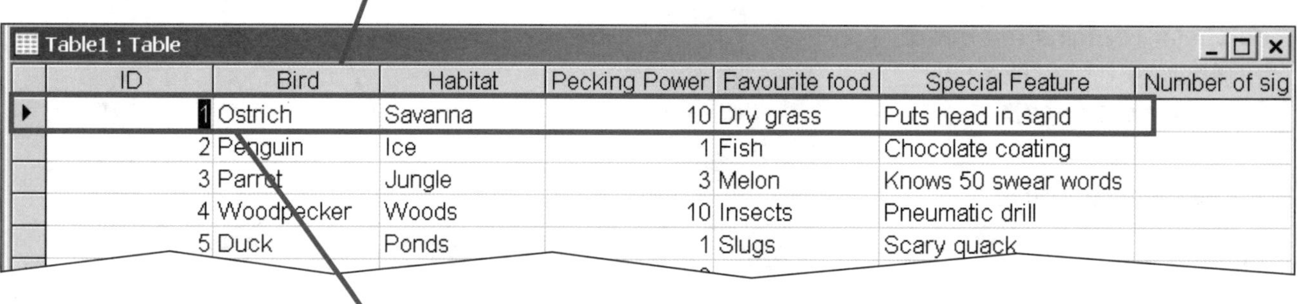

Table1 : Table

ID	Bird	Habitat	Pecking Power	Favourite food	Special Feature	Number of sig
1	Ostrich	Savanna	10	Dry grass	Puts head in sand	
2	Penguin	Ice	1	Fish	Chocolate coating	
3	Parrot	Jungle	3	Melon	Knows 50 swear words	
4	Woodpecker	Woods	10	Insects	Pneumatic drill	
5	Duck	Ponds	1	Slugs	Scary quack	

Each of these rows is a record. It has all the information about an individual entry. This record shows you all the information stored about the ostrich.

You've got a table, but no chairs...

I would make a joke about fields and records too, but quite honestly it wouldn't be very funny. Get these words clear in your head, because otherwise you'll get confused later on.

Database Basics

Get used to the way a database looks, and practise these basic skills...

You can Change Field Widths

Sometimes you have fields (columns) that are too wide, or too narrow to display your data:

Open the database 'Birds', and double-click on Table 1.

Move the mouse on to the dividing line between "ID" and "Bird", until it looks like this.

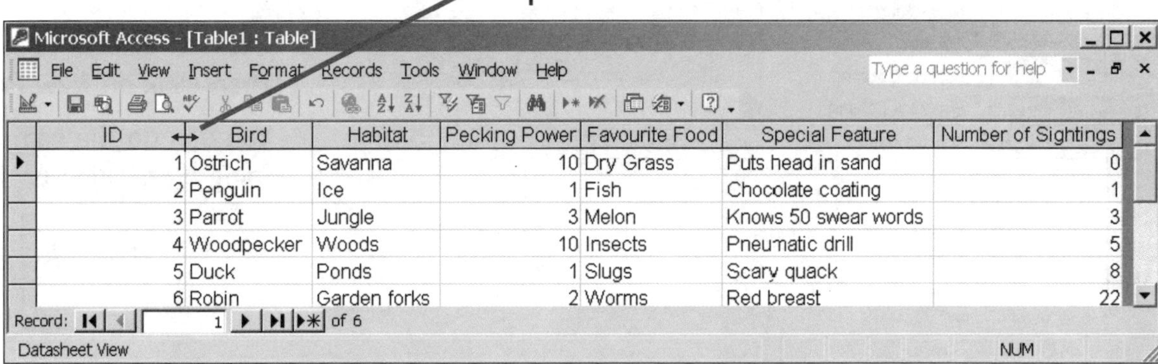

ID	Bird	Habitat	Pecking Power	Favourite Food	Special Feature	Number of Sightings
1	Ostrich	Savanna	10	Dry Grass	Puts head in sand	0
2	Penguin	Ice	1	Fish	Chocolate coating	1
3	Parrot	Jungle	3	Melon	Knows 50 swear words	3
4	Woodpecker	Woods	10	Insects	Pneumatic drill	5
5	Duck	Ponds	1	Slugs	Scary quack	8
6	Robin	Garden forks	2	Worms	Red breast	22

Double-click with the left mouse button, and the field will automatically resize to fit.

You can Move Between Records

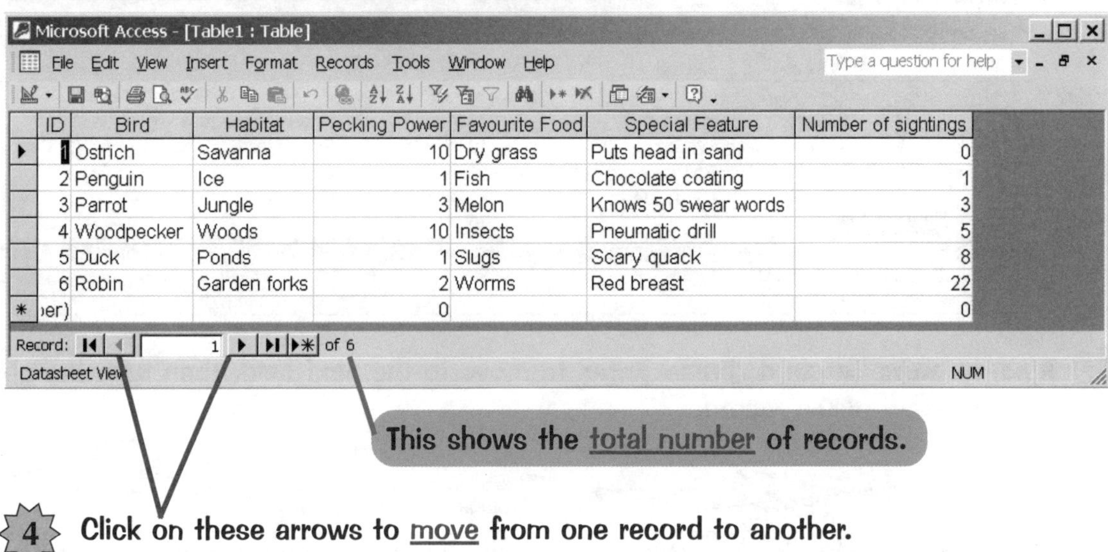

ID	Bird	Habitat	Pecking Power	Favourite Food	Special Feature	Number of sightings
1	Ostrich	Savanna	10	Dry grass	Puts head in sand	0
2	Penguin	Ice	1	Fish	Chocolate coating	1
3	Parrot	Jungle	3	Melon	Knows 50 swear words	3
4	Woodpecker	Woods	10	Insects	Pneumatic drill	5
5	Duck	Ponds	1	Slugs	Scary quack	8
6	Robin	Garden forks	2	Worms	Red breast	22
›er)			0			0

This shows the total number of records.

4 Click on these arrows to move from one record to another.

Now close the database.

Learn the basics and the rest will follow...

It might be simple, but it's important stuff, so don't be tempted to skip it. You need to know how to change the column widths or you won't be able to see your data properly.

Entering Data

You don't have to create a new database for the assessment — you just need to know how to add new records to an existing database. It's just a case of typing in the right place really.

Creating a New Record is Simple

 Open the database '<u>Birds</u>', and double-click on '<u>Table 1</u>'. You'll see something like this...

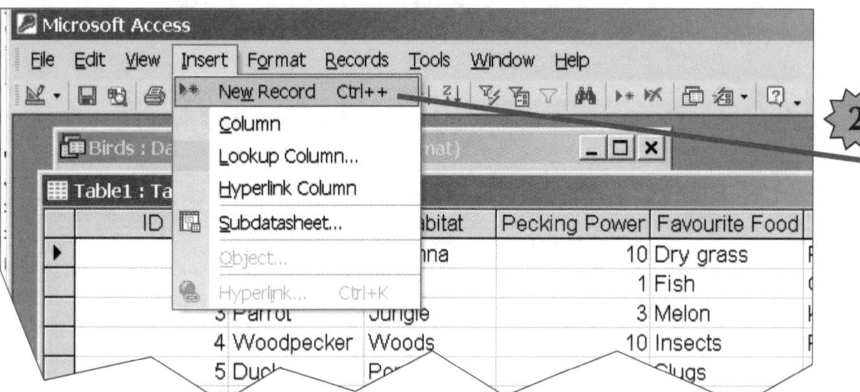

2 Click on insert.
Then click on New Record.

You can do the same thing by clicking on this button:

 A <u>new record</u> should appear at the bottom.
The first field will be <u>highlighted</u> and say '<u>Autonumber</u>'.

This means it'll fill in the record number <u>automatically</u>.
Press the '<u>Enter</u>' key to go to the next field.

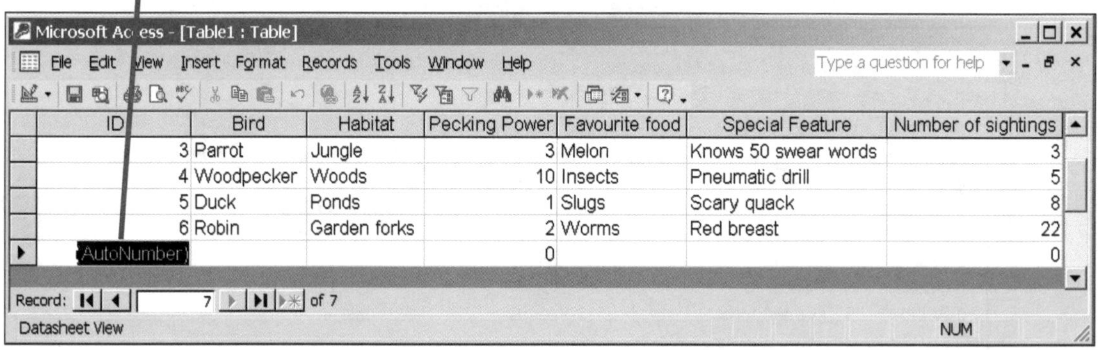

ID	Bird	Habitat	Pecking Power	Favourite food	Special Feature	Number of sightings
3	Parrot	Jungle	3	Melon	Knows 50 swear words	3
4	Woodpecker	Woods	10	Insects	Pneumatic drill	5
5	Duck	Ponds	1	Slugs	Scary quack	8
6	Robin	Garden forks	2	Worms	Red breast	22
(AutoNumber)			0			0

 Type the word 'Buzzard', press '<u>Enter</u>' to move to the next field, then type the <u>next</u> word. Fill in the rest of the record.

5	Duck	Ponds	1	Slugs	quack	8
6	Robin	Garden forks	2	Worms	Red breast	22
7	Buzzard	Moor	10	Carrion	Eats dead things	6
(AutoNumber)			0			0

5 Now <u>close</u> the database (your changes will be saved automatically).

New records are always added at the bottom...

New records are always added at the bottom — something which I'm sure won't upset you too much. If you feel you must change the order of your records, don't worry, you can sort them.

Amending Data

You're going to need to change the data in your database sometimes. Here's how to do it:

You can Change the Data in the Database

Imagine you've just found out that parrots actually prefer oranges to melons...

Open the database 'Birds', and double-click on 'Table 1'.

Click on the data you want to change — 'Melon'.

Table1 : Table

ID	Bird	Habitat	Pecking Power	Favourite food	Special Feature	Number of sightings
1	Ostrich	Savanna	10	Dry grass	Puts head in sand	0
2	Penguin	Ice	1	Fish	Chocolate coating	1
3	Parrot	Jungle	3	Melon	Knows 50 swear words	3
4	Woodpecker	Woods	10	Insects	Pneumatic drill	5
5	Duck	Ponds	1	Slugs	Scary quack	8
6	Robin	Garden forks	2	Worms	Red breast	22
7	Buzzard	Moor	10	Carrion	Eats dead things	6
(AutoNumber)			0			0

3 Delete 'Melon' (use the 'backspace' or 'delete' key) and type 'Orange' instead.

1	Ostrich	Savanna	10	Dry grass	Puts head in
2	Penguin	Ice	1	Fish	Chocolate co
3	Parrot	Jungle	3	Orange	Knows 50 sw
4	Woodpecker	Woods	10	Insects	Pneumatic dr
5	Duck	Ponds	1	Slugs	Scary quack

Now close the database 'Birds'.

It's as easy as falling off a log... (and it hurts much less)

When you add or amend data in 'Microsoft Access', it's automatically saved for you, so you don't have to remember to save it manually.

Deleting Records

Sooner or later you might need to delete things from your database. It's pretty straightforward:

You can Delete Records you don't Need

1. Open the database 'Birds', and double-click on 'Table 1'.

2. Click here to select the record you want to delete (the penguin).

Table1 : Table

ID	Bird	Habitat	Pecking Power	Favourite Food	Special Feature	Number of Sightings
1	Ostrich	Savanna	10	Dry Grass	Puts head in sand	0
2	Penguin	Ice	1	Fish	Chocolate coating	1
3	Parrot	Jungle	3	Orange	Knows 50 swear words	3
4	Woodpecker	Woods	10	Insects	Pneumatic drill	5
5	Duck	Ponds	1	Slugs	Scary quack	8
6	Robin	Garden forks	2	Worms	Red breast	22
7	Buzzard	Moor	10	Carrion	Eats dead things	6
...er)			0			

3. Press the 'Delete' key once.

4. If you're sure you're deleting the right record, click 'Yes'.

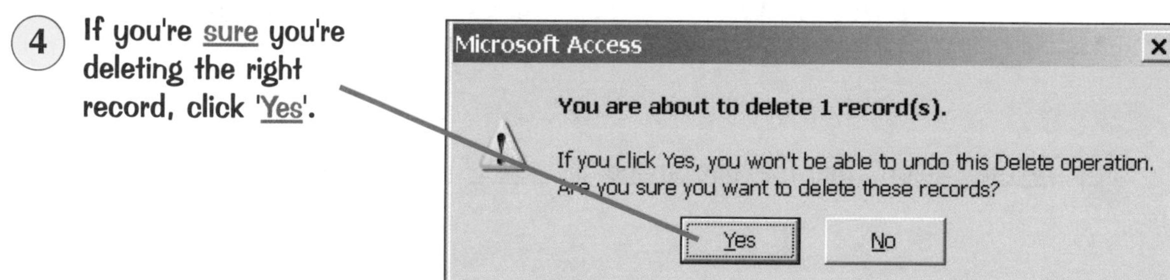
Microsoft Access
You are about to delete 1 record(s).
If you click Yes, you won't be able to undo this Delete operation.
Are you sure you want to delete these records?
Yes
No

Table1 : Table

ID	Bird	Habitat	Pecking Power	Favourite food	Special Feature	Number of sightings
1	Ostrich	Savanna	10	Dry grass	Puts head in sand	0
3	Parrot	Jungle	3	Orange	Knows 50 swear words	3
4	Woodpecker	Woods	10	Insects	Pneumatic drill	5
5	Duck	Ponds	1	Slugs	Scary quack	8
6	Robin	Garden forks	2	Worms	Red breast	22
7	Buzzard	Moor	10	Carrion	Eats dead things	6
...er)			0			0

Ta da — the penguin record's gone.

The ID field is not renumbered — you've lost ID 2 for good.

Deleting gives me a real power-trip...

If I delete someone from my database, do they cease to exist?
Hmmm... manipulation of data is a powerful thing, so think before you delete anything.

Deleting Records

There's an easy way to delete a whole block of records if you need to.

You can Delete Lots of Records at once

Click on the first record you want to delete.

Press 'Shift' and hold it down.

Table1 : Table

	ID	Bird	Habitat	Pecking Power	Favourite food	Special Feature	Number of sightings
	1	Ostrich	Savanna	10	Dry grass	Puts head in sand	0
▸	3	Parrot	Jungle	3	Orange	Knows 50 swear words	3
	4	Woodpecker	Woods	10	Insects	Pneumatic drill	5
	5	Duck	Ponds	1	Slugs	Scary quack	8
	6	Robin	Garden forks	2	Worms	Red breast	22
	7	Bu	Moor			Eats dead things	6
*							0

Click on the last record you want to delete.
This selects the first record, last record, and any in between.

Table1 : Table

	ID	Bird	Habitat	Pecking Power	Favourite food	Special Feature	Number of sightings
	1	Ostrich	Savanna	10	Dry grass	Puts head in sand	0
▸	3	Parrot	Jungle	3	Orange	Knows 50 swear words	3
	4	Woodpecker	Woods	10	Insects	Pneumatic drill	5
	5	Duck	Ponds	1	Slugs	Scary quack	8
	6	Robin	Garden forks	2	Worms	Red breast	22
	7	Buzzard	Moor	10	Carrion	Eats dead things	6
*	ber)			0			0

4 Now press 'Delete'.
You'll see this window.

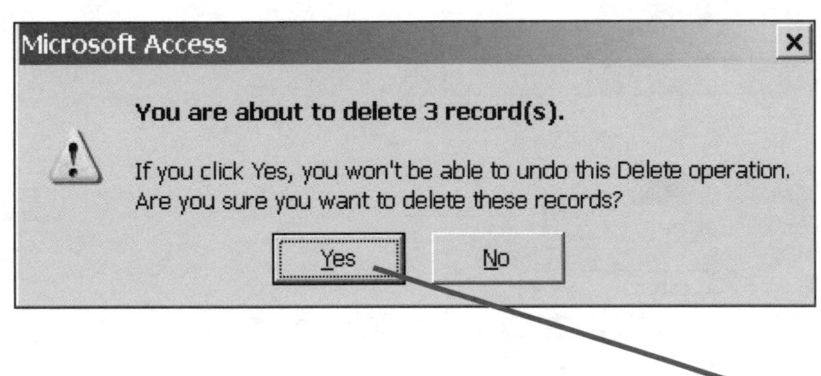
Microsoft Access
You are about to delete 3 record(s).
If you click Yes, you won't be able to undo this Delete operation.
Are you sure you want to delete these records?
Yes
No

If you're sure you want to delete the selected records, click 'Yes'.

Deleted items are gone forever...sob...

Be really careful when you delete things in 'Microsoft Access'. Because it saves your changes automatically, once you delete records you can't get them back again.

Find and Replace

If you want to change a piece of data that occurs throughout a table, you need to use 'Find and Replace' — it'll save you loads of time and hassle.

Find and Replace is really Quick

Open the database 'Stock Records' and double-click on Table 1.

Click here to select the 'Location' field.

Janet didn't tell her boss how quick 'Find and Replace' was.

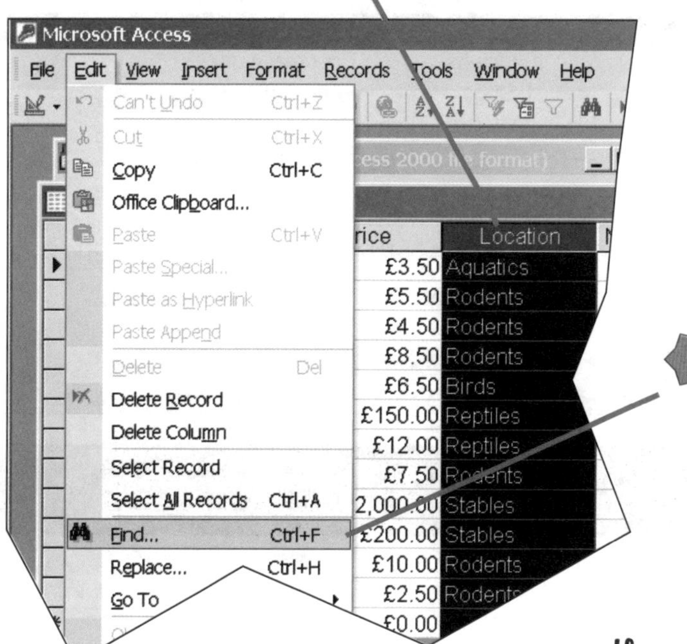

3 Click on 'Edit', then on 'Find'...'

Or you can just click on the 'Find' button:

If you are using Access 97 this is a bit different: Click on 'Edit', then on 'Replace'...' and skip straight to point 5.

You'll see this window:

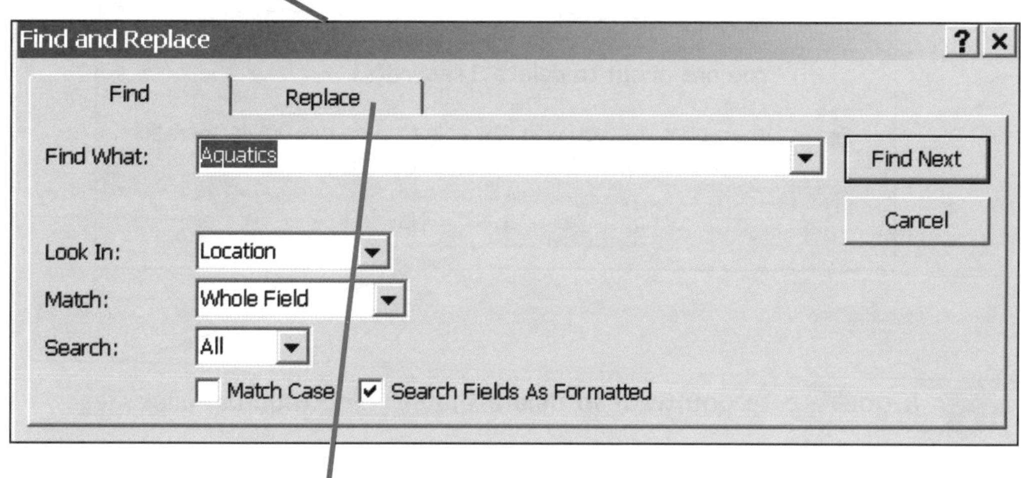

4 Click on the 'Replace' tab to bring it to the front.

Find and Replace

5 Type the word you want it to find here — 'Rodents'.

6 Type the words you want to replace it with here — 'Small Mammals'.

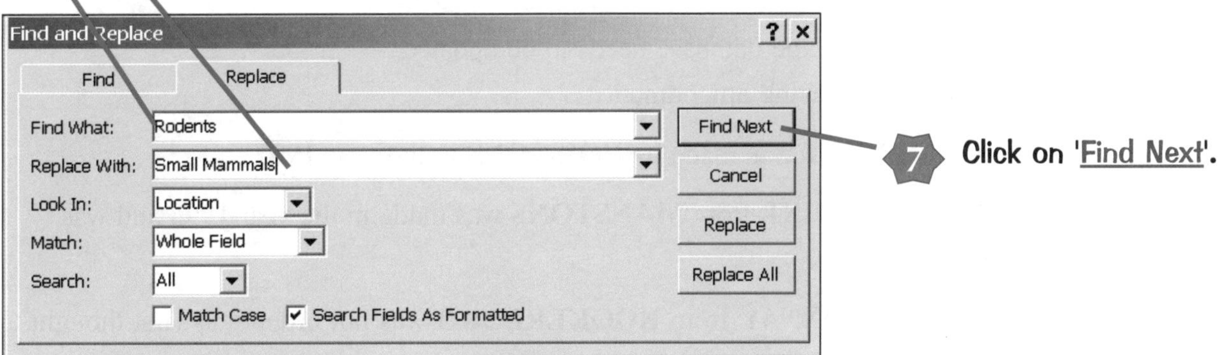

7 Click on 'Find Next'.

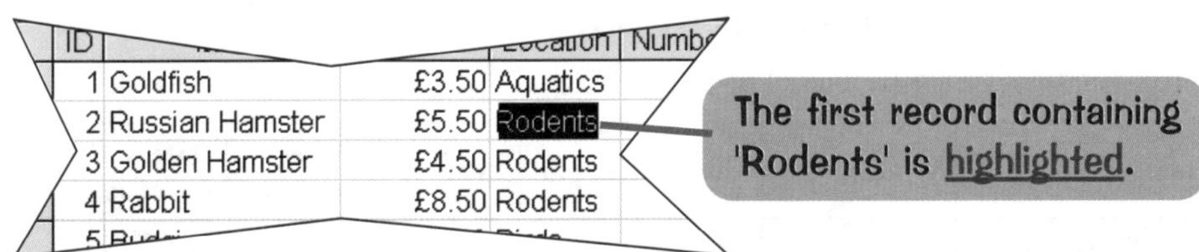

The first record containing 'Rodents' is highlighted.

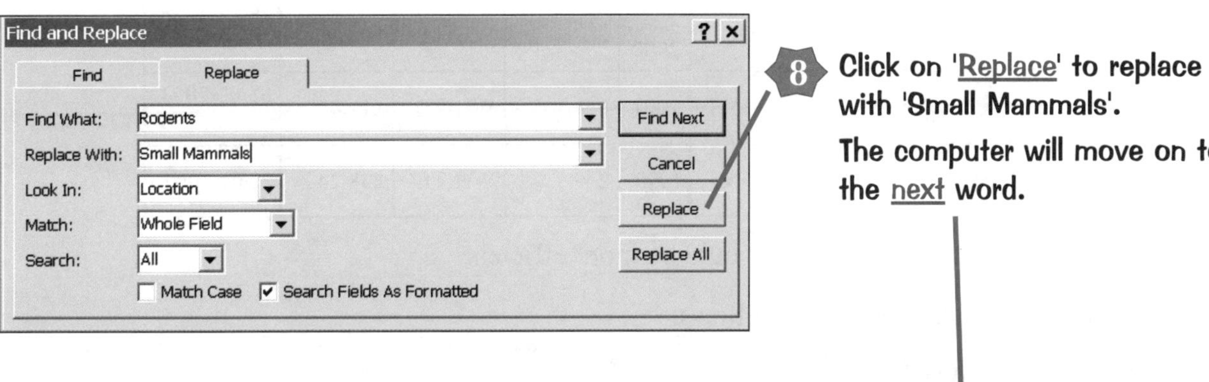

8 Click on 'Replace' to replace it with 'Small Mammals'.

The computer will move on to the next word.

9 Repeat until you've changed all of the entries.

Once you're sure the computer is changing the right data, you can click 'Replace All' — the computer will change all the words at once.

It's easy to replace things...

Don't forget to use Find and Replace in the assessment. It's well worth learning it, rather than changing each record individually. That's how data-entry errors happen...

Section Three — Practice Exercises

It's time to practise changing, deleting and adding data... bet you can't wait...

Exercise 1

1. Open the database **Wines**.
2. Some of the information in the database needs to be updated.
   You need to make the following amendments:
   a) Wine **5556 MERLOT** was made by **ROISTONS** in the year **1997**.
   b) Wine **5562 MUSCADET** from **MANSTONS** was made in the year **1990** and was **£102.28** per case.
3. The wine **5563 CHARDONNAY** from **KOOKERBORO** was not ordered as first thought. Delete this record from the database.
4. Four cases of wine have recently been purchased.
   Create records for the four new cases as follows:

WineID	Name	Winery	Year	Strength	Type	Price per case	Date of Purchase
5567	CHATEAU NEUF DE PAT	ROISTONS	1988	2	RED	£57.82	02/03/2003
5568	MUSCADET	PAY D'OC	2000	2	WHITE	£93.91	03/12/2002
5569	CHARDONNAY	ROISTONS	2001	1	WHITE	£11.49	03/03/2003
5570	MUSCADET	ROISTONS	1999	2	WHITE	£38.24	12/01/2003

5. Using codes in the **TYPE** field would be more efficient.

   Replace the existing entries as follows:

   a) Replace **WHITE** with **W**

   b) Replace **RED** with **R**

   c) Replace **SPARKLING** with **S**

   d) Replace **FORTIFIED** with **F**

Section Three — Practice Exercises

We've thoughtfully provided another page of practice for you, just to show that we care.

Exercise 2

1. Open the database **Equipment**.

2. Some of the information in the database needs to be updated.
You need to make the following amendments:

    a) The **KODAK SLIDE PROJECTOR KIT** (EQUIPMENT ID **12**) should be of **AUDIO VISUAL** type.

    b) The **REALISTIC TELESCOPIC STAND** (EQUIPMENT ID **18**) was bought on **14/05/2001** with a cost of **30**.

3. The Equipment ID **4 (YAMAHA GRAPHIC EQUALISER)** was not bought as first thought.
Delete this record from the database.

4. Four new pieces of equipment have recently been purchased.
Create records for the four new pieces of equipment as follows:

EQUIPMENT ID	MANUFACTURER	DESCRIPTION	TYPE	SIZE	PURCHASE DATE	PURCHASE COST
23	FLASH	STROBE CONTROLLER	LIGHTING	SMALL PORTABLE	26/04/2003	399
24	JEM	SMOKE MACHINE	LIGHTING	LARGE	24/05/2003	1250
25	FLASH	MIRROR BALL	LIGHTING	SMALL PORTABLE	15/03/2003	200
26	FLASH	LINEAR STROBE LIGHT	LIGHTING	SMALL PORTABLE	18/07/2003	250

5. Using codes in the **TYPE** field would be more efficient.

    Replace the existing entries as follows:

    a) Replace **SOUND** with **SO**

    b) Replace **COMMUNICATIONS** with **CM**

    c) Replace **AUDIO VISUAL** with **AV**

    d) Replace **LIGHTING** with **LG**

Database Queries

In databases, you can find records that match certain criteria — for example, in a zoo database you could find all the animals that eat cheese and weigh more than a tonne. Amazing.

Making Queries Means Asking Questions

Queries are about asking your database questions. There are loads of really complex queries you can do, but for New CLAIT, all you have to learn about is:

Matching words — e.g. finding all the people in a database with the hair colour 'brown'.

Comparing numbers — e.g. finding all the people who are taller than 6 ft.

Here's How to Make a Simple Query

Queries are probably the hardest part of New CLAIT. But don't worry we'll build up slowly by starting with a really simple query — here goes...

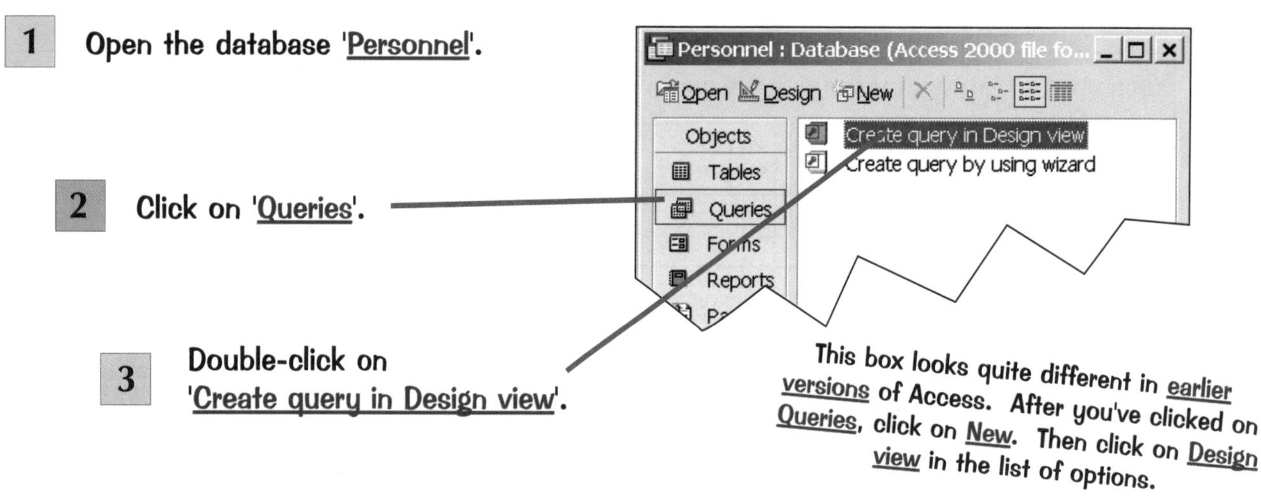

1 Open the database 'Personnel'.

2 Click on 'Queries'.

3 Double-click on 'Create query in Design view'.

This box looks quite different in earlier versions of Access. After you've clicked on Queries, click on New. Then click on Design view in the list of options.

4 You'll see a window like this — it's where you select which tables to use.

There's only one here so just make sure it's selected, and click on 'Add'.

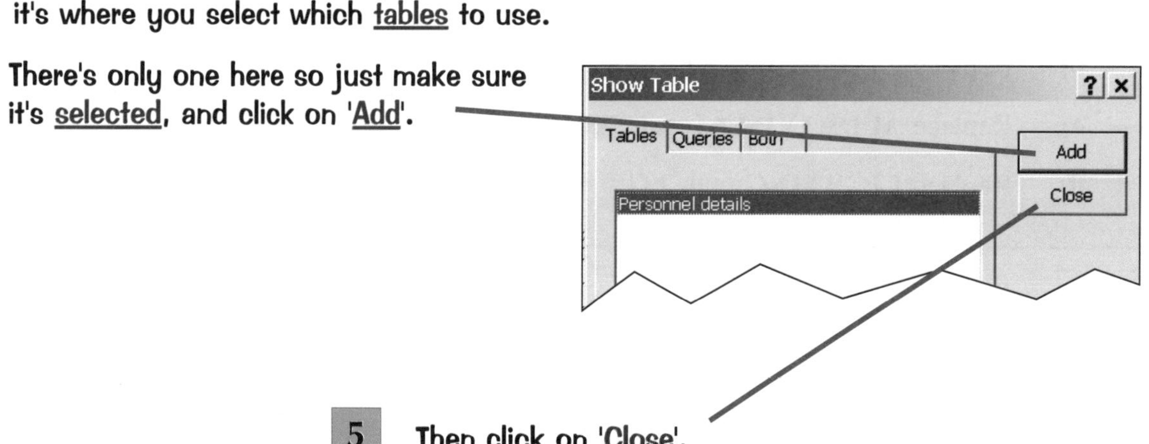

5 Then click on 'Close'.

Database Queries

Keep reading, you're not finished yet...

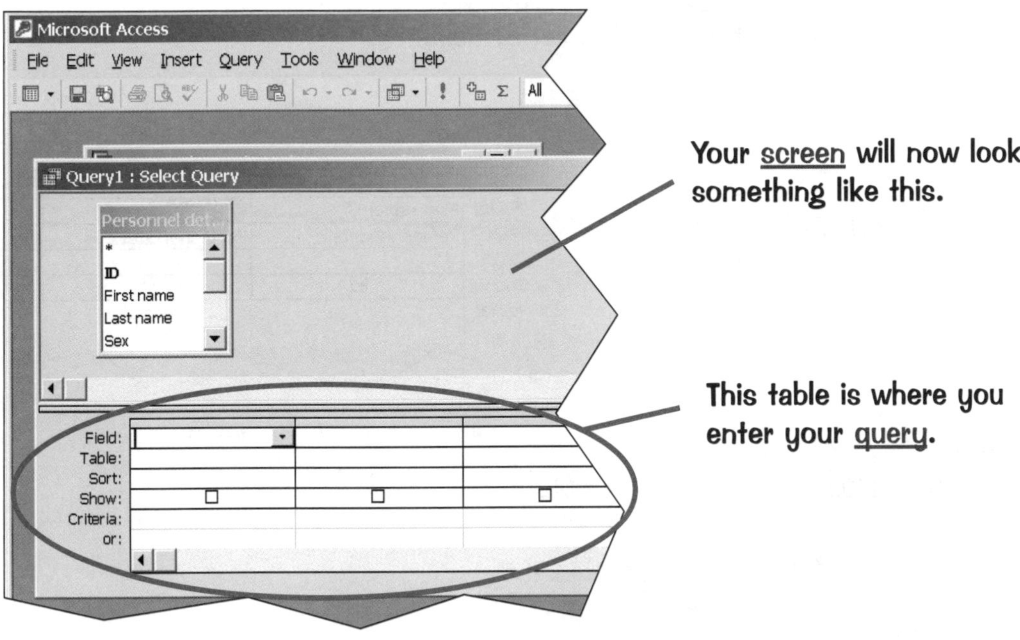

Your screen will now look something like this.

This table is where you enter your query.

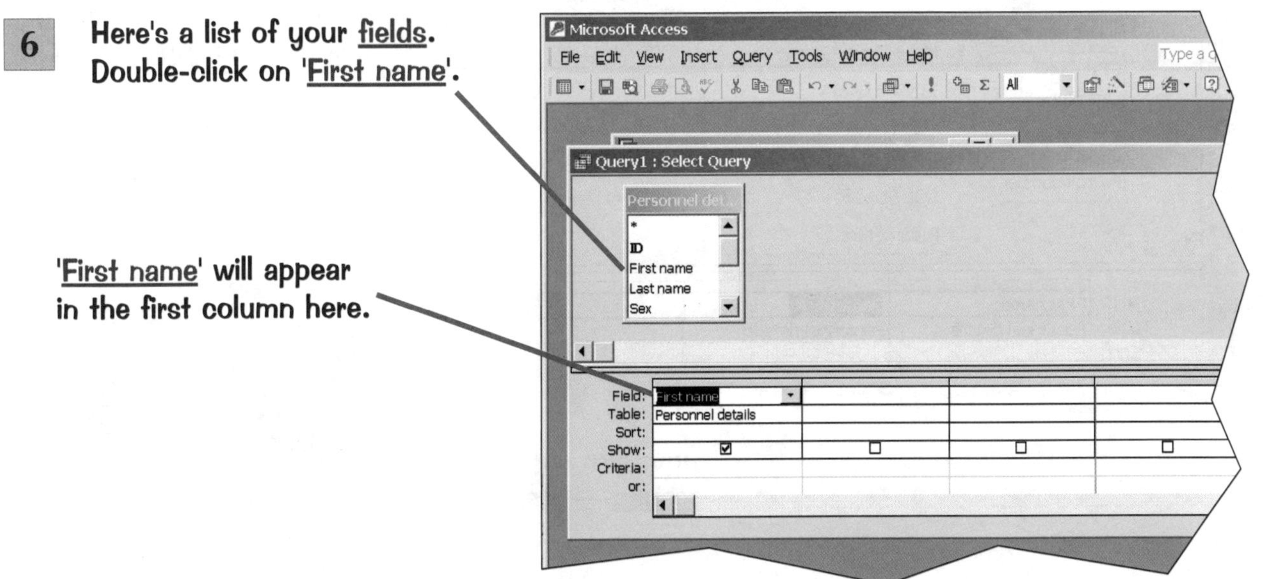

6 Here's a list of your fields. Double-click on 'First name'.

'First name' will appear in the first column here.

You've now told the database that you'd like to see the information in the 'First name' field.
But you also want to see information in the 'Department' field...

...Keep reading, there's still more...

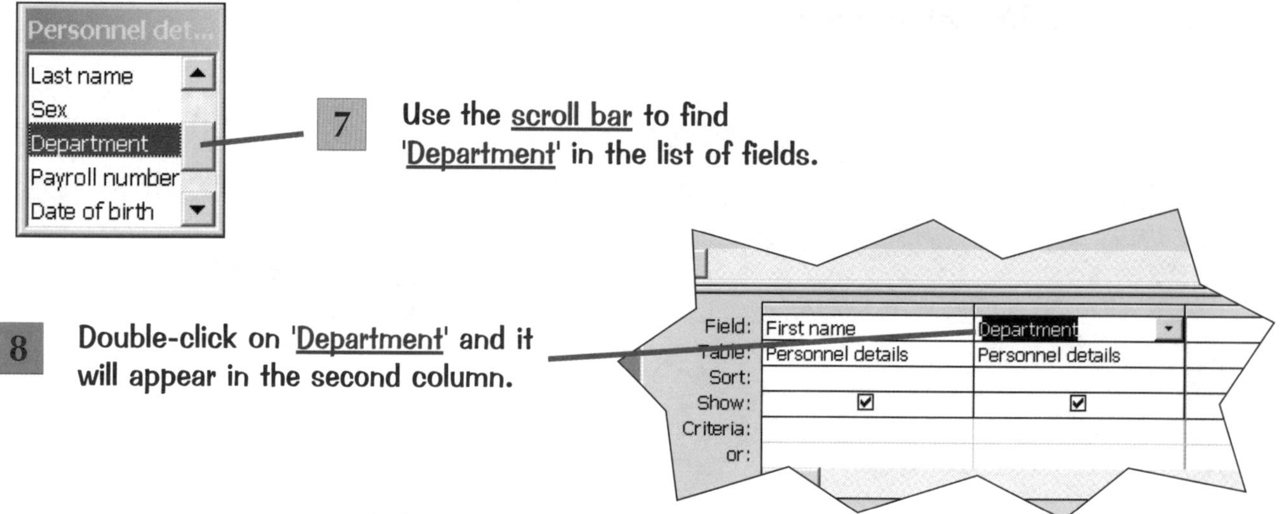

7 Use the scroll bar to find 'Department' in the list of fields.

8 Double-click on 'Department' and it will appear in the second column.

So you've asked the database to show you a list of first names, and the departments those people work in.

Microsoft Access

File Edit View Insert Query Tools Window Help

Run
Show Table...
Remove Table
Select Query
Crosstab Query
Make-Table Query...
Update Query
Append Query...
Delete Query
SQL Specific
Parameters...

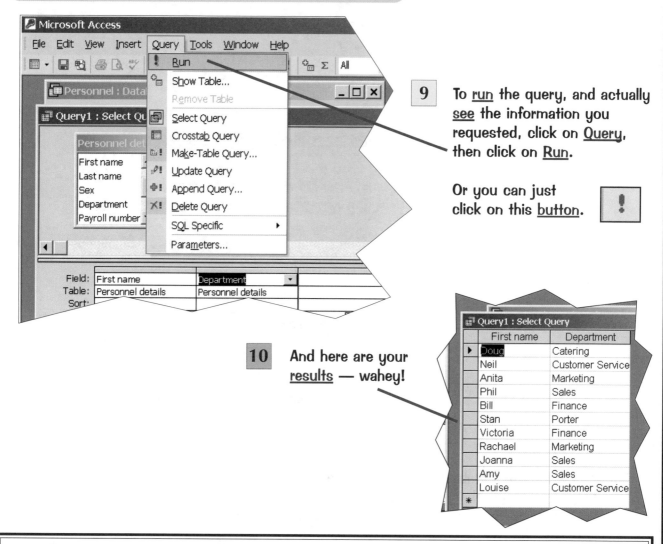

9 To run the query, and actually see the information you requested, click on Query, then click on Run.

Or you can just click on this button.

10 And here are your results — wahey!

Query1 : Select Query

First name	Department
Doug	Catering
Neil	Customer Service
Anita	Marketing
Phil	Sales
Bill	Finance
Stan	Porter
Victoria	Finance
Rachael	Marketing
Joanna	Sales
Amy	Sales
Louise	Customer Service

Make a query — ah go on, go on, go on...

You might think you could have just read those results from the table. Well, that's true, but this little exercise is just what you need for practice before we move on to more complex queries...

Database Queries

Now you know how to do fairly basic queries, here's how to do some nice complex ones.

Some Queries Can be Really Useful...

We're going to be using the 'Personnel' database again — here's a good meaty query:

Which women earn £13,000 or more?

1. Follow steps 1 to 5 from page 22 to open up a new query window.

2. You want to know the names of the women, so double-click on 'First name' in the little box.

3. You want to know which people are women, so double-click on 'Sex'.

4. You want to compare them on how much they earn, so double-click on 'Salary'.

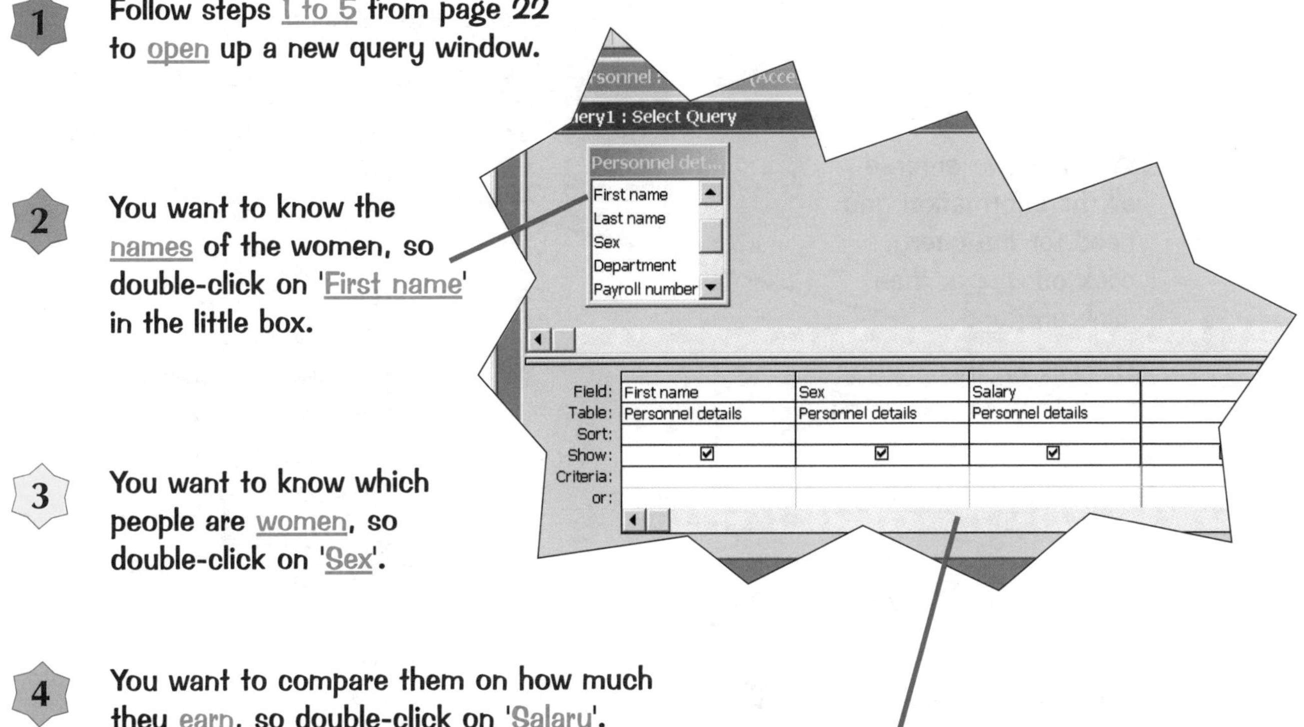

You'll end up with three columns filled in like this.

If you ran the query now, you'd just get lists of all the people, their sex and their salary — but databases are a lot cleverer than that. For each field, you can select criteria, so you can choose what you want to see, like Sex = Female.

5. You only want to see the data on women, so type an F into the 'Criteria' row of the 'Sex' column.

   This basically finds all the people in the database with an F for 'Sex' — the women.

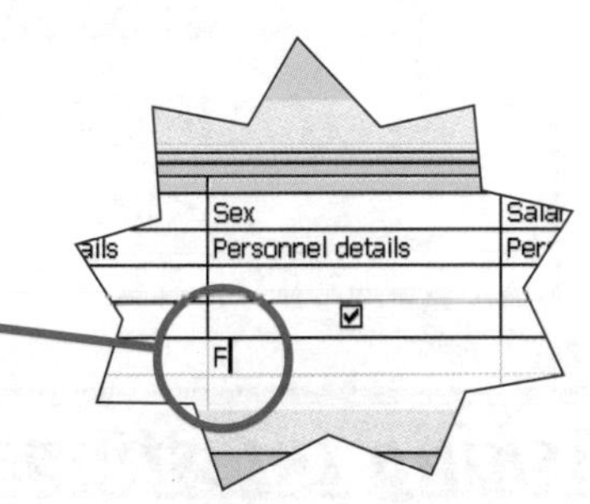

Turn the page for the rest...

Database Queries

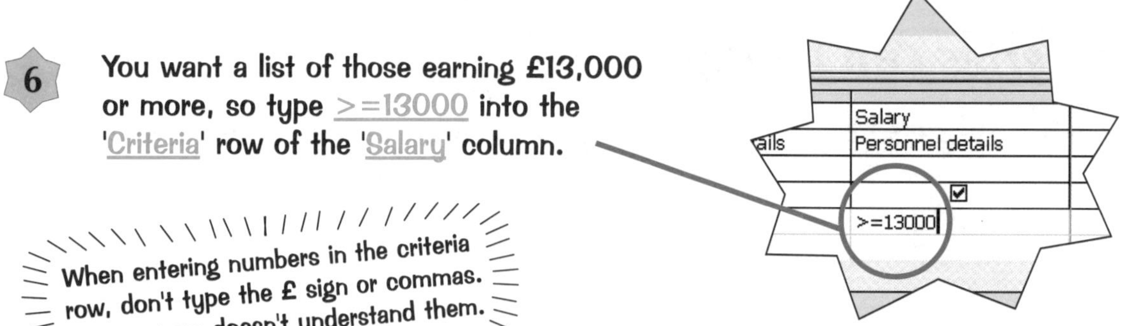

6 You want a list of those earning £13,000 or more, so type >=13000 into the 'Criteria' row of the 'Salary' column.

When entering numbers in the criteria row, don't type the £ sign or commas. The program doesn't understand them.

Don't worry for the minute what '>=' means — keep reading and all will be explained...

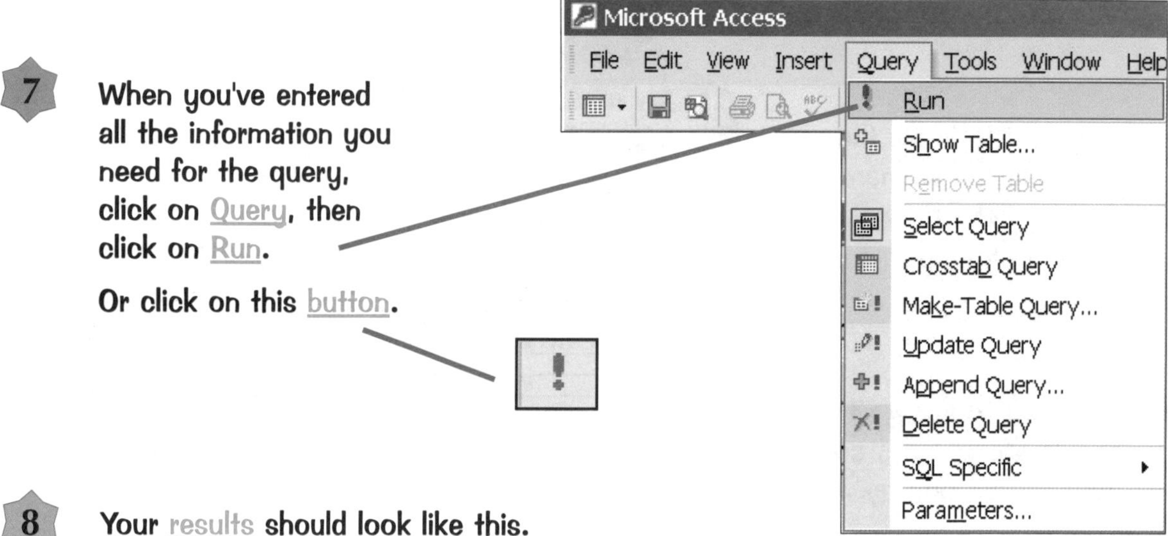

7 When you've entered all the information you need for the query, click on Query, then click on Run.

Or click on this button.

8 Your results should look like this.

It's a list of all the women who earn £13,000 or more — just what you wanted.

	First name	Sex	Salary
▶	Anita	F	£18,000.00
	Joanna	F	£13,000.00
	Amy	F	£21,000.00
	Louise	F	£15,000.00
*			£0.00

Remember typing in >=13000? Well, here's what it's all about:

=13000 looks for records with a value equal to 13,000.

>=13000 looks for records with a value of greater than or equal to 13,000.

<=13000 looks for records with a value of less than or equal to 13,000.

>13000 looks for records with a value of greater than 13,000.

<13000 looks for records with a value of less than 13,000.

Asking questions has never been so much, erm, fun..

My advice to you is just to have a play — what's the worst that could happen? After you've made a couple of queries, it'll all suddenly fall into place. And then think how smug you'll feel...

Displaying Query Results

With these clever little tricks, you'll be able to display query results in properly useful ways.

You Can Choose Which Fields to Display

When you did the query on the last page, you might have thought there was no point in displaying the 'Sex' field — it didn't tell you anything new or interesting...

You can choose to not display the 'Sex' field:

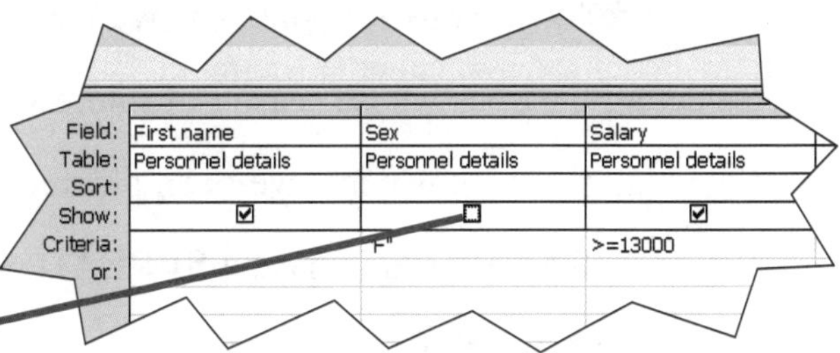

1. Follow steps 1 to 6 from the last worked example.

2. In the 'Sex' column, just click in the box on the 'Show' row to untick it.

3. Run the query as before (see page 26).

The same query will run, but you won't see the 'Sex' field in the results.

You Can Show Your Query Results in Order

You can put your query results in ascending or descending alphabetical, numerical or date order.

With the example from above, it would be useful to see the salaries in ascending order...

1. Do the query above, but don't click on the 'Run' button yet.

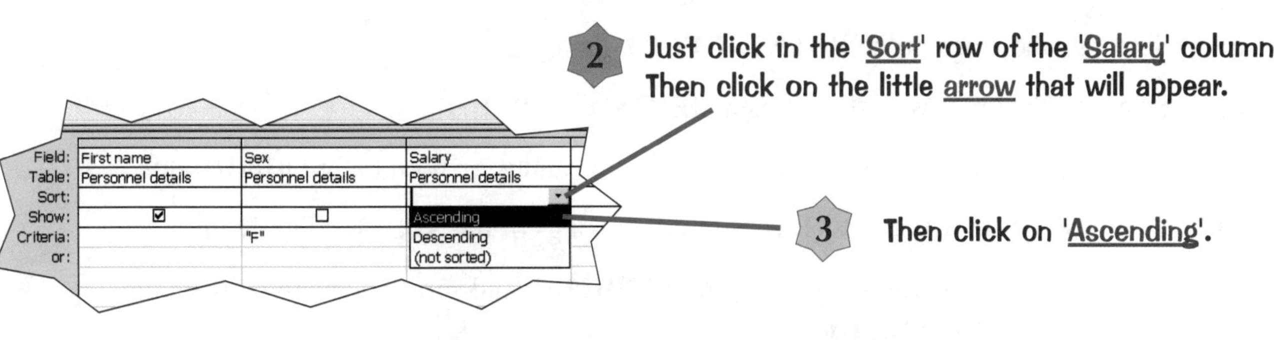

2. Just click in the 'Sort' row of the 'Salary' column. Then click on the little arrow that will appear.

3. Then click on 'Ascending'.

4. Run the query as before (see page 26).

Now your results will appear, but this time they'll be in order.

There's nowt as queer as queries...

You can even sort dates into order, just be careful — ascending order by date would put the earliest date first, through to the latest date — give it a try, it's the best way to learn.

Section Four — Practice Exercises

Right then, now it's time to see what you've learnt... Ooh, so many questions...

Exercise 1

1. Open the database **Trees**.
2. Do the following queries (start a new query for each one):
   a) Select all the trees whose season of interest is **WINTER**.
   b) Select all the trees which have been planted after **01/01/1980**.
   c) Select all the trees which have a **SPREAD** of less than **15m** and a **HEIGHT** of less than **20m**.
   d) Select the **LATIN NAMES** of all the trees which were planted after **01/01/1960**. Sort them into ascending alphabetical order of **LATIN NAME**.
   e) Select all the trees with a spread of less than **23m** and a height of more than **12m**. Sort the results into ascending order of **HEIGHT**, but do not show the data for **SPREAD**.
   f) Show the **NAMES** and **LATIN NAMES** of the trees in ascending order of **HEIGHT**, but do not show the data for **HEIGHT**.
3. Exit the software.

Exercise 2

1. Open the database **Royals**.
2. Do the following queries (start a new query for each one):
   a) Select all the kings of the **PLANTAGENET** family line.
   b) Select all the kings who started their **REIGN** after **01/01/1300**.
   c) Select all the kings who had less than **6** children and were born before **01/01/1400**.
   d) Show the **MOTHER** and **FATHER** of all the kings of the **STUART** family line.
   e) Select all the kings who were born after **01/01/1100**, and sort the data into ascending alphabetical order of **NAME**.
   f) Select all the kings of the **STUART** family line who had more than **4** children. Show the **NAME** and **CHILDREN** fields only.
3. Exit the software.

Section Four — Practice Exercises

It's not over quite yet... Just two more exercises and then you can make a nice cup of tea.

Exercise 3

1. Open the database **Wines**.
2. Do the following queries (start a new query for each one):
   a) Select all **WHITE (W)** type wines.
   b) Select all wines costing less than **£70** per case.
   c) Select all the wines with a **STRENGTH** of more than **2**, whose **YEAR** was before **1999**.
   d) Select all the wines from the **MANSTONS** winery, with a price of more than **£50** per case.
   e) Select all the **WHITE (W)** type wines purchased after **01/02/2003**.
   Sort the data into alphabetical order of **NAME**, but don't show the data for **TYPE**.
   f) Select the **NAME**, **WINE ID** and **YEAR** of all the wines with a strength of less than **3**.
   Sort the data into descending order of **YEAR**, but don't show the data for **STRENGTH**.
3. Exit the software.

Exercise 4

1. Open the database **Equipment**.
2. Do the following queries (start a new query for each one):
   a) Select the **DESCRIPTION** of all equipment purchased **after 01/01/2001.**
   b) Select the **DESCRIPTION** of all equipment which is **LARGE** in size.
   c) Select the **DESCRIPTION** of all equipment which is of type **SOUND (SO)** and was bought for less than **£100**.
   d) Show the **EQUIPMENT ID** of all **MICROPHONE**s which cost more than **£50**.
   Don't show the data for **DESCRIPTION**.
   e) Select the **DESCRIPTION** and **PURCHASE COST** of all equipment of type **SOUND (SO)** which was purchased before **01/02/2001**. Sort the data into ascending order of **PURCHASE COST**.
   f) Show the **MANUFACTURER** of all equipment of type **LIGHTING (LG)**.
   Sort the data into alphabetical order of **MANUFACTURER**. Don't show the field for **TYPE**.
3. Exit the software.

Sorting Data

This page shows you how to sort your data — a clever way to make life easier.

Sorting Data Makes it Easier to Understand

When you're looking through a table, you might find it makes more sense if the records appear in some sort of order. Say, alphabetical order of surname...

1. Open the database 'Personnel', then open the 'Personnel details' table.

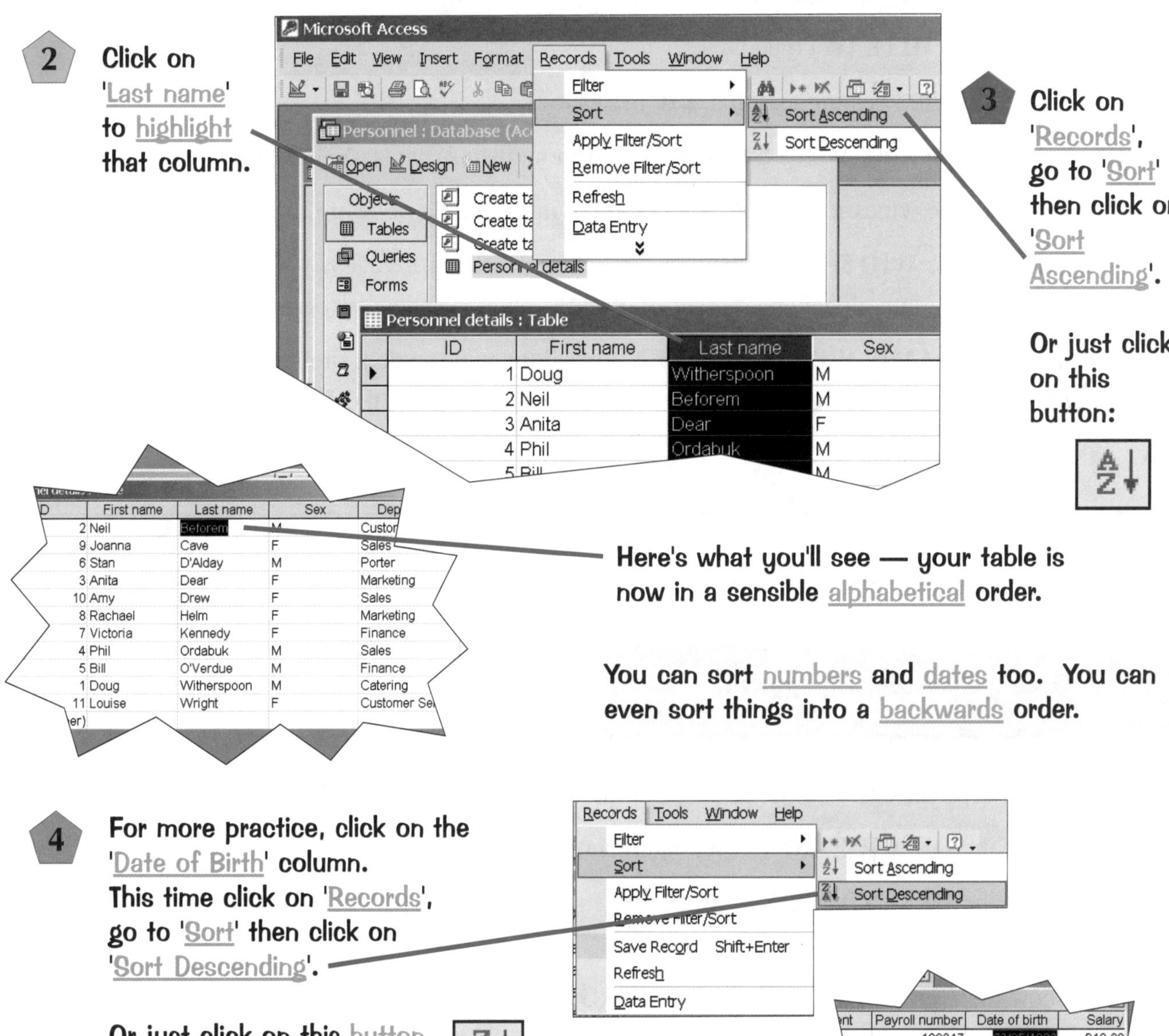

2. Click on 'Last name' to highlight that column.

3. Click on 'Records', go to 'Sort' then click on 'Sort Ascending'.

Or just click on this button:

Here's what you'll see — your table is now in a sensible alphabetical order.

You can sort numbers and dates too. You can even sort things into a backwards order.

4. For more practice, click on the 'Date of Birth' column. This time click on 'Records', go to 'Sort' then click on 'Sort Descending'.

Or just click on this button.

Here's what you'll get — the records are now in descending order of date of birth. Youngest first, that is.

Sort your life out — use a database...

With such small tables, it might not be entirely obvious why sorting is so very useful. Just imagine having 5,000 records in a database, though. Then you'll find sorting pretty handy.

Filtering Data

Filtering is another handy trick you should get to grips with.

Filtering Data is Quite Useful Too

Filtering is a little like querying. It lets you select a piece of information from your database, and then shows all the records with that same piece of information. Like so:

1. Open the 'Personnel details' table (if you haven't already).

Say you wanted to see the records for all the people in Sales...

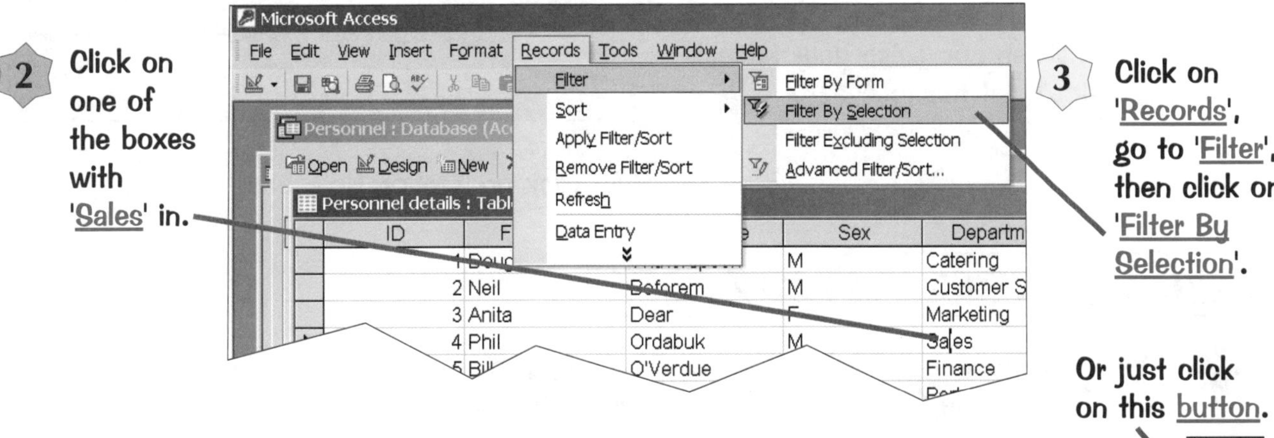

2. Click on one of the boxes with 'Sales' in.

3. Click on 'Records', go to 'Filter', then click on 'Filter By Selection'.

Or just click on this button.

4. Look at what happened — now you've only got the records for people in Sales. Perfect.

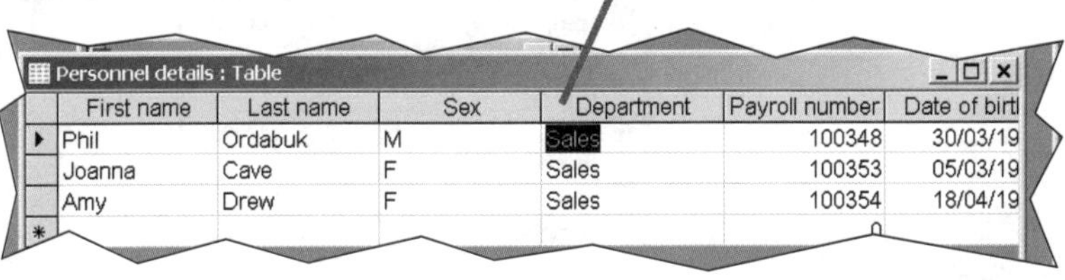

Personnel details : Table

	First name	Last name	Sex	Department	Payroll number	Date of birt
▸	Phil	Ordabuk	M	Sales	100348	30/03/19
	Joanna	Cave	F	Sales	100353	05/03/19
	Amy	Drew	F	Sales	100354	18/04/19
*					0	

5. Remove the filter — go to 'Records' and click on 'Remove Filter/Sort' or click on this button.

Here's another chance to practise. This time you want to see all the men.

6. Click on one of the boxes with 'M' for male in.

7. Filter the data again as you did in step 3.

8. And hey presto — here are all the men in the table.

	Sex	Department	Payroll number	Date
▸	M	Porter	100350	
	M	Finance	100349	
	M	Customer Service	100346	
	M	Sales	100348	
	M	Catering	100345	
*			0	

Try not to filter out the boring bits...

Think how useful this could be if you had thousands of medical records, but only wanted to see the people with athlete's foot. Two simple clicks and there they are. Foot fungus and all.

Saving Tables and Queries

Ah, this is an easy page. You should know how to save stuff already, so this won't be too bad.

Tables Save Automatically

When you add new records, or amend your data, your changes get saved automatically. So when you close your table, you won't get a message asking if you want to save.

But... If you make changes to the table's presentation, (e.g. by sorting, filtering or changing column widths), these changes won't save automatically...

...When you close your table, you'll get this message.

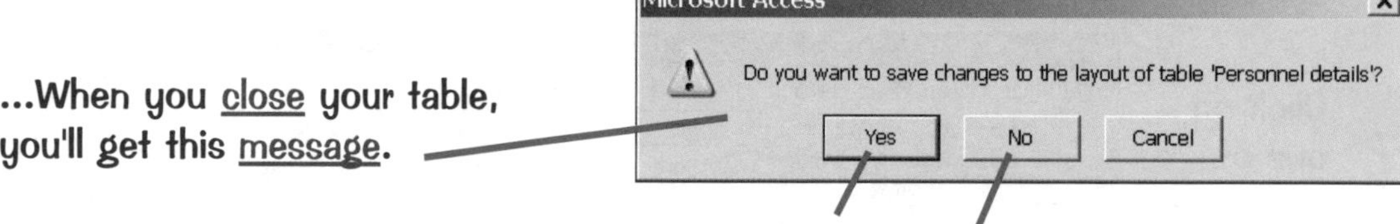

Just click on 'Yes' or 'No'. Easy as that.

Saving Queries is Pretty Easy

1. Open the 'Personnel' database and make a query to find the favourite fruits of people who work in Sales.

2. Click on 'File', then on 'Save'.

3. You'll get a little window like this. Choose a name for your query and type it here.

4. Click on 'OK'.

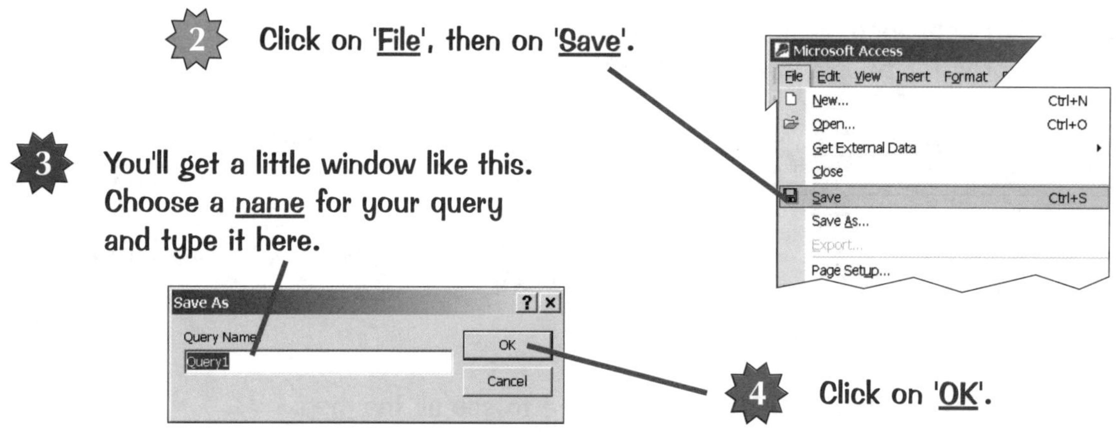

When you saved your query, you didn't get a choice of where to save it... That's because your query is saved as part of your database.

Your saved queries end up in this window here. You can open them by double-clicking on them here.

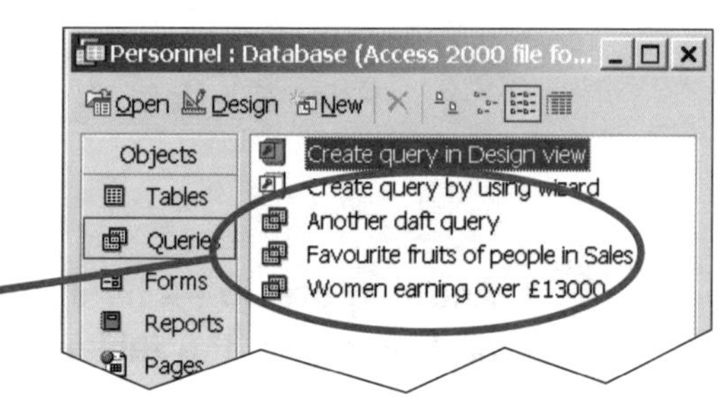

Saving them? Whatever next...

If you did a query which listed all the people who liked oranges, then a new person joined the company who liked oranges, they would be automatically added to the list of results. So the database updates your queries with any new data entered in the database — now that's clever.

Printing Tables and Queries

Printing. Where stuff from your screen turns up on paper. A wonder of modern technology...

You Can Print Tables, if You Fancy

Printing tables is just like printing anything really.

1. Open the 'Personnel' details table.

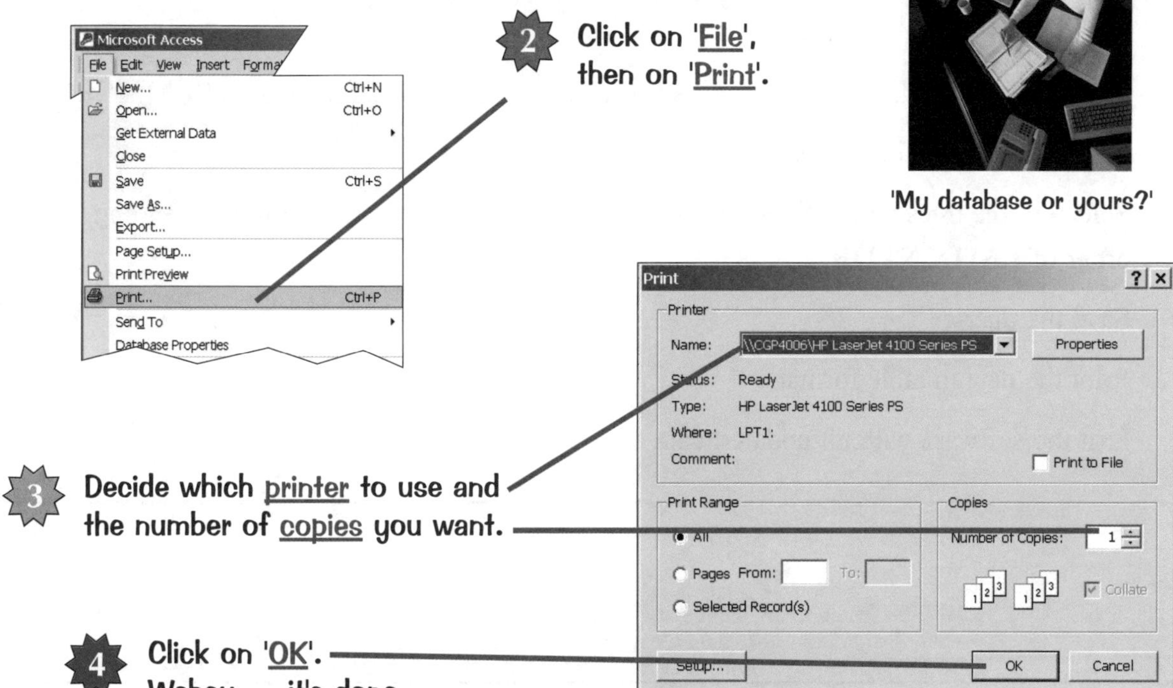

'My database or yours?'

2. Click on 'File', then on 'Print'.

3. Decide which printer to use and the number of copies you want.

4. Click on 'OK'. Wahey — it's done.

Printing Queries isn't Much Different

You can print queries in just the same way as printing tables.
To print a query:

1. Open a saved query.

2. Follow steps 2 to 4 from above.

Erm... that's it. Easy as chicken nuggets.

Some things you print might not fit nicely on a sheet of paper.
To see how your printout will look, just click on this button.
When you've finished looking, just close the window.

Have fun printing — but remember the trees...

Printing is something you should make sure you get to grips with. You can guarantee you're going to have to print lots of things in your assessment, and if you can't, well, that's it. Sorry.

Section Five — Practice Exercises

Here's a little something for you... What fun — another couple of practice exercises.

Exercise 1

1. Open the database **Trees**.
2. Sort the data into ascending order of date **PLANTED**.
3. Print the data in table format.
4. Filter the data to show all the records for trees whose season of interest is **SUMMER**.
5. Print the data in table format.
6. Select all the trees with a **SPREAD** of **20m** or less, and sort the data into ascending order of **LATIN NAME**.
7. Save the query.
8. Print the data in table format.
9. Exit the software with all updated data saved.

Exercise 2

1. Open the database **Royals**.
2. Sort the data into descending order of date **STARTED REIGN**.
3. Print the data in table format.
4. Filter the data to show all the records for kings of the **STUART** family line.
5. Print the data in table format.
6. Select all the kings who had more than **6 CHILDREN** and were **BORN** after **01/01/1200**. Sort the data into ascending order of **NAME**.
7. Save the query.
8. Print the data in table format.
9. Exit the software with all updated data saved.

Section Five — Practice Exercises

And some more... Don't worry, it's nearly over now.

Exercise 3

1. Open the database **Wines**.
2. Sort the data into descending order of **YEAR**.
3. Print the data in table format.
4. Filter the data to show all the records for wines from the **ROISTONS** winery.
5. Print the data in table format.
6. Select all the wines with a **STRENGTH** of less than **3**, whose **YEAR** was **1999** or before. Sort the data into ascending order of **PRICE** per case.
7. Save the query.
8. Print the data in table format.
9. Exit the software with all updated data saved.

Exercise 4

1. Open the database **Equipment**.
2. Sort the data into ascending order of **MANUFACTURER**.
3. Print the data in table format.
4. Filter the data to show all the records for equipment from the manufacturer **YAMAHA**.
5. Print the data in table format.
6. Select all equipment which is of type **SOUND** (**SO**) and was bought for more than **£100**. Sort the data into ascending order of **PURCHASE COST.**
7. Save the query.
8. Print the data in table format.
9. Exit the software with all updated data saved.

Advice for the Assessment

So you're thinking about the assessment? Then this is the page for you.
A whole page of handy assessment hints, and warnings about things you'll want to avoid doing.
And if you keep reading, you'll also find a useful checklist and practice assessment. Wow.

You'll get 2 Hours to Complete the Assessment

You've got plenty of time to do the assessment, so...

- Don't panic.
- Don't rush — you'll make mistakes.
- Read the instructions properly, and make sure you follow them.
- Check your work as you go along, especially your typing.
- Don't panic. (Did I mention that already?)

Avoid these Errors

If you make a major error, you won't pass. Major errors include failing to do one of the tasks in the assessment, like selecting the wrong data in a query, or not printing the specified fields. So, make sure you follow the instructions carefully.

If you make more than three minor errors, you won't pass the assessment either.
So, avoid making small mistakes like these:

1) Making a typing (data entry) error in the text you're asked to enter.
2) Using capital letters in an inconsistent manner.
3) Deleting part of a record instead of deleting the whole record.
4) Failing to sort data in the correct manner.
5) Failing to include field headings on a printout.
6) Not showing all the data on a printout through having the wrong column widths.

Watch Out for Data Entry Errors

When you're asked to type something, make sure you type it exactly as it's written, with the right spacing and punctuation — otherwise you're just throwing easy marks away.

Print your documents to check for errors, then correct them on the computer before you hand them in.

Just take a few deep breaths and you'll be fine...

It's quite important to find out what classes as a major or minor error. Watch out for those minor errors or a few silly little errors could stop you passing your assessment.

Advice for the Assessment

Here's a little something to help you work out what you know. See how much you can tick off...

Check that you Know How to Do These Things

All you need to know to pass the assessment is in this book.
Use the checklist below to make sure you're confident with all the tasks you could be asked to do. Go back and look at the relevant pages again if you're not sure.

(Don't tick the boxes unless you're confident you could do the tasks in an exam situation.)

1)	Open a saved database and table.	☐	Pages 10-11
2)	Open a saved table.	☐	Page 12
3)	Change the widths of columns (fields).	☐	Page 13
4)	Enter new data into a table.	☐	Page 14
5)	Amend existing data in a table.	☐	Page 15
6)	Delete a record, or a group of records.	☐	Pages 16-17
7)	Make amendments using 'Find and Replace'.	☐	Pages 18-19
8)	Make a query based on one or two criteria.	☐	Pages 22-26
9)	Use <, >, <= and >= in queries.	☐	Page 26
10)	Choose which fields to display in the results of queries.	☐	Page 27
11)	Sort query results into alphabetical, numerical or date order.	☐	Page 27
12)	Sort data in tables into alphabetical, numerical or date order.	☐	Page 30
13)	Filter tables to show only certain data.	☐	Page 31
14)	Save tables and queries.	☐	Page 32
15)	Print tables and queries.	☐	Page 33

You're nearly there, keep going... not far now...

If you've ticked all the boxes, you should be ready for the assessment.
But wait, what's this? A practice assessment over the page? Aren't you lucky.

Section Six — Practice Assessment

You've got to the end of the book — quite an achievement really. Not long ago, databases were pretty alien things, but now you can open them, change them, add things to them and use them to find stuff out. (Don't get too smug yet though, you've still got a practice assessment to go.)

Scenario

You are working as an administrative assistant for Premier Consultants.
Your job includes looking after a database of specialist consultants in the north west.

Your manager has asked you to amend the database of consultants and provide some routine reports.

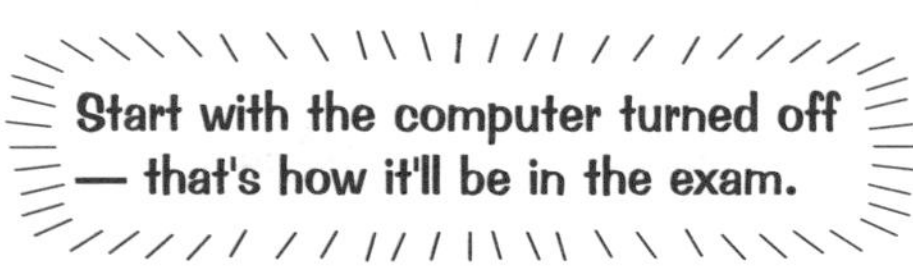
Start with the computer turned off
— that's how it'll be in the exam.

1. Switch on the computer and monitor correctly and safely.
   Wait for the operating system to load fully.
2. Open the database **Consultants**.
3. Using codes in the **Specialism** field would be more efficient.
   Replace the existing entries as follows:
   a) Replace **Databases** with **DB**.
   b) Replace **Networks** with **NT**.
   c) Replace **Accounting** with **AC**.
   d) Replace **Graphics** with **GR**.
   e) Replace **Project Management** with **PM**.
4. **Hull** from Preston is no longer working for the company. Delete this record from the database.
5. Four new consultants have recently joined Premier Consultants.
   Create records for the four new consultants as follows:
   a) **White** from the town of **Bolton** started on **04/03/2004**. He is available for **6** days, his preference is **any day**, car is **yes** and specialism is **NT**.
   b) **Fernandez** from **Preston** started on **02/02/2004**. She is available for **2** days, her preference is **weekend**, car is **no** and specialism is **GR**.
   c) **Chang** from **Manchester** started on **24/03/2004**. He is available for **5** days, his preference is **any day**, car is **no** and specialism is **PM**.
   d) **Burns** from **Liverpool** started on **02/02/2004**. She is available for **3** days, her preference is **weekday**, car is **yes** and specialism is **DB**.

Section Six — Practice Assessment

6. Some of the information in the database needs to be updated.
You need to make the following amendments:

a) **Thompson** now lives in **Preston** and is available for **2** days.

b) The start date for **George** should be **03/12/2002** and car is now **yes**.

7. Print all the data in table format, making sure all the records are fully visible.

8. The company would like to offer consultancy services to new businesses that have started up recently. Set up the following database query:

a) Select all consultants whose start date is after **01/04/2002**.

b) Sort the data in ascending order of **start date**.

c) Display only the **surname**, **start date**, **specialism**, **preference** and **car** fields.

d) Save the query.

e) Print out the results of the query in table format.

9. There has been a lot of interest in network specialism from businesses that want a consultant to advise in new areas of network installation. Set up the following database query:

a) Select all consultants for whom car is **yes** and whose **specialism** is **NT**.

b) Sort the data in descending order of **days available**.

c) Display only the **surname**, **town**, **preference** and **days available** fields.

d) Save the query.

e) Print the results of the query in table format.

10. The company needs to know whether or not to recruit more consultants to cope with the demand for consultancy services. Set up the following database query:

a) Select all consultants whose **days available** is more than **2**.

b) Sort these records into ascending order of **specialism**.

c) Display only the **surname**, **town**, **specialism**, **preference** and **car** fields.

d) Save the query.

e) Print the results of the query in table format.

11. Exit the software with all updated data saved.

Index